NEW-FANGLED LICKETY-SPLIT DEVOTIONS

JANE —
Lickety-Split
Joy in Jesus,
my friend!
"Dr. Devo"

by Tim Wesemann
Illustrations by Dana Thompson

Zonder**kidz**

We want to hear from you. Please send your comments about this book to us in care of zreview@zondervan.com. Thank you.

Zonder**kidz**.

The children's group of Zondervan

www.zonderkidz.com

Dr. Devo's New-Fangled Lickety-Split Devotions
Copyright © 2004 by Tim Wesemann

Requests for information should be addressed to:
Grand Rapids, Michigan 49530

ISBN: 0–310–70697–1

Library of Congress Cataloging-in-Publication Data

Wesemann, Tim, 1960-
    Dr. Devo's new-fangled lickety-split devotions / written by Tim
Wesemann ; illustrated by Dana Thompson.–1st ed.
        p. cm.
    ISBN 0-310-70697-1 (pbk.)
    1. Children—Prayer-books and devotions—English. 2. Christian
education of children. I. Title: Doctor Devo's new-fangled
lickety-split devotions. II. Thompson, Dana. III. Title.
    BV4870.W47 2004
      242'.62-dc22
    2004008457

Editor: Bruce Nuffer
Interior design: Susan Ambs
Art direction: Laura Maitner

Printed in the United States of America

04 05 06 07 08/❖ DC/5 4 3 2 1

Dedicated (along with special thanks) to all the kids who answered Dr. Devo's questions which include classes from the following schools and churches . . .

Salem Lutheran School - Affton, MO
VBS at United Methodist Church of Windsor, MO
Green Park Lutheran School - Lemay, MO
VBS at First Christian Church - Windsor, MO
Kid ministry groups at Messiah Lutheran Church - Midland, MI
Lutheran School Association, Cole Camp, MO
Messiah Lutheran School, St. Charles, MO
St. Luke's Lutheran Sunday School, Tillsonburg, Ontario, Canada
St. James Lutheran Church/School Quincy, IL

. . . as well as individuals in:

St. Louis, MO	Fort Worth, TX
Oakville, MO	Moscow, Russia
Fenton, MO	Broken Arrow, OK
Wishek, ND	Texas City, TX
St. Charles, MO	House Springs, MO
Prairie Village, KS	A small town in GA
Pflugerville, TX	Chesterfield, MO
Cole Camp, MO	Bradenton, FL
Munster, IN	Manchester, MO
Imperial, MO	Minnetonka, MN

. . . and any others I didn't mention who helped, edited, prayed for, or encouraged Dr. Devo and D.J.! You are all appreciated!

INTRODUCTION

What's "newfangled" about *Dr. Devo's Newfangled, Lickety-Split Devotions?* Sara from Minnetonka (yes, that's really the name of a city) wrote me a letter. She was very kind to tell me how much she enjoyed *Dr. Devo's Lickety-Split Devotions.* Sara said it taught her how fun devotions can be!

Learning about God's love through Jesus should be fun! That's why I, Dr. Devo, (short for "devo"tions) and my lab assistant D.J. (Devo Junior) love creating fun, Bible-centered devotions in our lab!

What's newfangled about this book is that kids helped write it! I asked hundreds of kids questions, and their answers are part of almost every devotion! I learned so much from the great answers they gave. Through the power of the Holy Spirit, so will you! We can learn so much from kids your age. D.J. and I thank God for your faith and witness. Have fun growing in God's awesome love for you!

Remember this newfangled truth from the New Testament:

> Don't let anyone look down on you because you are young, but set an example for the believers in speech, in life, in love, in faith and in purity.
>
> 1 TIMOTHY 4:12

Why is the Bible so long?

(A) God wouldn't stop talking. (Chad)

(B) Because it has lots of pages. (Correna)

(C) Because it tells of everyone who is important, and that's a lot! (Katy)

(D) It is long because God's Word does not stop. (Lydia)

Which answer do you think is closest to being correct? Each answer makes some sense or at least makes you smile. But check out this verse from the Old Testament:

The grass withers and the flowers fall, but the word of our God stands forever.

Isaiah 40:8

That may not be exactly what Lydia meant with her answer, but it is true that God's Word doesn't stop—it won't die, go away, or change. It has truth that will last forever and is good for the entire world!

I, Dr. Devo, want you to always remember these truths from God's Word: God loves you, he forgives you through Jesus' death and resurrection, and he will take all who base their faith and life in Jesus to live with him forever. His Word and promises will never end! Say it out loud:

"God loves me! He forgives me! I'll live with him forever! His Word never ends!"

Say it again: "God loves me! He forgives me! I'll live with him forever! His Word never ends!"

Do you think Jesus had a favorite miracle?

There are so many miracles to choose from! Jesus walked on water. He raised people from the dead. He made the lame walk and the deaf hear. It is even a miracle that he would have D.J. and me write all these devotions! Do you have a favorite?

But Jesus wouldn't have a favorite, would he? He might. Jesus mentions something very important in the short story of Zacchaeus. You can read about it in Luke 19:1–10.

Check out that last verse, "The Son of Man came to seek and to save what was lost." The reason Jesus (the Son of Man) came to earth was to save us. We are sinners. We haven't done anything to deserve his love. But Jesus came to save us by dying on the cross and then rising from the dead. Whoa! That's some miracle! Definitely Dr. Devo's favorite! Maybe it's Jesus' favorite and yours too!

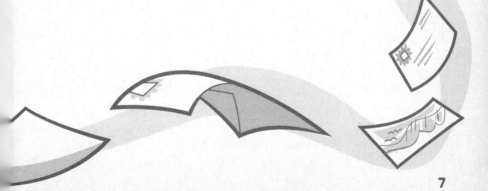

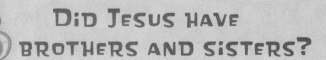

DID JESUS HAVE BROTHERS AND SISTERS?

About half the kids didn't think Jesus had brothers and sisters. Actually, he did. Mark 6:1–6 tells the story of Jesus' coming to his hometown with his disciples. It mentions Jesus' brothers: James (not the disciple), Joseph (or Joses), Judas (not the disciple), and Simon (not Simon Peter, the disciple). It also mentions his sisters, but it doesn't give their names.

Here are some of the other kids' answers:

- He would probably always be correcting me.

- It would be awesome. He would never get mad or anything.

- I'd be sad that he got crucified.

- It would be good. You could pray to your brother.

So what would it be like to have Jesus as a brother? You may not have to imagine it because Jesus once said, "Whoever does God's will is my brother and sister" (Mark 3:35). He is your brother! Is that cool or what?

LOL!
(Laughing Out Loud)

Q: Why did the peanut go into the ocean?

A: He wanted to be with the jellyfish.

I love peanut butter and jelly sandwiches! D. J. loves peanut butter and cheese sandwiches. (He's a little odd!) In Matthew's joke, the peanut would go all the way into the ocean to be with the jellyfish.

How far would you go to be with someone? Would you go to the ocean? Walk to the mountains from your house? Run to the desert?

Would you walk outside the city limits to a cross, in order to die for someone? Whoa! Go to a cross? That's what Jesus did for us, so that we could be forgiven and live

> Let us fix our eyes on Jesus, the author and perfecter of our faith, who for the joy set before him endured the cross.
>
> HEBREWS 12:2

forever with him. He went to a grave to defeat death. He faced the devil and won! He went to heaven to prepare a place for us. What a Savior! What a friend! What a love! That's how far Jesus went to be with us!

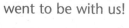

9

WHAT WOULD YOU LIKE TO ASK JESUS?

In Matthew 7:7 Jesus says, "Ask and it will be given to you." Wow! Ask for anything? Hey Jesus, I want a million dollars. D.J. wants "A's" on all his tests at Lab Assistant School—without having to study!

Wait a minute. That doesn't sound right. I guess as we read that verse, we should remember that in other parts of the Bible, Jesus teaches us to ask for things according to his will. He wants what is best for us. Asking for a million dollars might not be what is best for us. And D.J. shouldn't get an "A" without using the brain God gave him.

What would you like to pray for, asking that God's will be done? Don't forget to listen for his answers! Here are some serious and some silly questions other kids had:

- What does heaven look like?

- How old are you now?

- Why does my dog keep hopping over the fence?

- And Kirsten would ask:

  How many grains of sand are in the Sahara desert? (Because that's the only question her dad can't answer.)

WHAT'S THE GREATEST PLACE IN THIS WORLD THAT GOD CREATED AND WHY?

I found some hot-weather kids giving answers like:

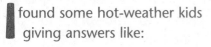

- The Bahamas

- California—it is hot

- Jamaica, because it is really warm and it has a lot of beaches

- Florida, because it's hot and relaxing

- The patriotic kids said America is the greatest place on earth.

Several kids thought the greatest place was church. That sounds like what King David wrote: "I'm asking the Lord for only one thing. Here is what I want. I want to live in the house of the Lord all the days of my life. I want to look at the beauty of the Lord. I want to worship him in his temple (Psalm 27:4 NIrV).

Thank the Lord for all of his creation as you think about your answer to this question!

Hey Moses—
I have a question!

Sara told me that if she could ask someone from the Bible a question, she would like to know exactly how it felt for Moses to lead all those people through the parted Red Sea.

Moses led probably two million people out of Egypt, through the wilderness, and to the promised land. That's a lot of responsibility! I have trouble keeping up with D.J.! Add to that the fact that they walked right through the Red Sea as God parted the waters before them. They walked through a miracle!

> God said [to Moses],
> "I will be with you.
> EXODUS 3:12

But that's not the end of the story. Even after all they had seen, the people started complaining to Moses about God. Their complaining caused them to miss out on the great plans God had for them.

Do you realize that you are walking through miracles right now? God parts the sun and moon and makes day and night—every 24 hours. He keeps your heart beating and your body growing! Don't be a complainer. Thank God for all the miracles that are taking place in your life. And trust him—no matter what!

Blessed are those whose sins are _____.

Everyone had the right answer! Forgiven! Blessed is he whose transgressions are forgiven (Transgression is another word for "sin")! Those are words from Psalm 32:1. I'm so glad everyone I interviewed knew that answer.

David is the one who wrote those words in Psalm 32. He knew all about God's forgiveness. He knew he was blessed to have been forgiven. He didn't deserve it, and neither do we!

Now God calls us to forgive others as we have been forgiven. Jesus took our place on the cross and died so we can be forgiven for all our sins. That's going to lead us to forgive others.

- We are blessed because we are forgiven by Jesus, our Savior!

- We can be a blessing to others by forgiving them!

- If God forgives us, we can forgive ourselves and others!

- We don't deserve his love and forgiveness, but it is ours! Never forget that or stop being happy because of it!

KiDS WiTH CANCER
(FiRST OF SiX)

When I'm not working in my laboratory to invent new devotions, one of the things I like to do is visit a children's hospital to share the good news of Jesus with some of the kids who have cancer.

When Jeremiah was asked, "If you could tell other kids about your illness, what would you tell them?" he answered, "I would tell them that they can't catch it."

I'm guessing some people have stayed away from visiting Jeremiah or getting close to him because they think they can catch his cancer. Seeing hospitals, oxygen masks, and wheelchairs could cause them to think that way. Just the same, you can't catch cancer from others. That might not be the case with some other illnesses though. It's best to check with your parents.

Once you've cleared it with your parents, go visit the kids you know with cancer and other illnesses. Pray for them. Play with them too! Talk to them. Spend time with them. Laugh with them. Cry with them. Love them. Caring is catching. Cancer isn't.

Consider visiting someone in the hospital or at home who needs a friend as you read this verse from 2 John 12: "I have much to write to you, but I do not want to use paper and ink. Instead, I hope to visit you and talk with you face to face, so that our joy may be complete."

KiDS WiTH CANCER
(SECOND OF SIX)

I asked Tyler, who has cancer, "What do you believe about Jesus?" He answered, "Jesus is God's Son, and he can heal people."

That's a great answer! He is God's Son, the world's Savior. But Tyler also needed to know that Jesus can heal people—that he's bigger than cancer or any other illness. Throughout Jesus' life on earth he healed many people, proving that he has power over sickness.

But what about when people die? Do you wonder why Jesus didn't heal them? Don't forget about this. If a person dies believing in Jesus as their personal Savior, that person will be perfectly healed in heaven! No more running noses, shots, flu, hospitals, cancer, or death.

> When Jesus landed and saw a large crowd, he had compassion on them and healed their sick.
>
> MATTHEW 14:14

Sometimes Jesus heals people while they are here on earth. And sometimes he heals by taking them to heaven and giving them a new, flawless body. The important thing to remember is what Tyler says, "He is God's Son, and he can heal people."

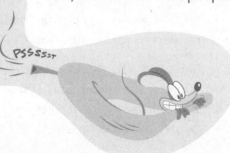

PSSSSST

Have you ever spent time in the hospital? Kids with cancer often have to spend a lot of time there getting treatments, having tests, and just waiting. So I asked some kids with cancer, "What's the silliest thing someone has said or done while you've been in the hospital?" We both laughed at Tyler's response, "I hate it when people say, 'It doesn't hurt that bad!'"

"It doesn't hurt that bad!" Has anyone ever said that to you? Maybe you wanted to yell back, "Oh yeah? How do you know? It's my body and I felt it! Believe me, it hurt!"

We have a great high priest. ... He is Jesus the Son of God. ... We have a high priest who can feel it when we are weak and hurting. ... So let us boldly approach the throne of grace. Then we will receive mercy. We will find grace to help us when we need it.

HEBREWS 4:14–16 (niRv)

Some people don't think it hurt that bad when Jesus was crucified. Yeah right! Nails were driven through his body, he was beaten with a whip, a crown of thorns was pressed onto his head. Jesus hung on the cross, gasping for breath, dying.

Still people say things like, "He's God—it didn't hurt that bad for him." Jesus was 100 percent human and 100 percent God. Believe it—he hurt. He knows what it's like when we hurt. He cares. He understands. And he promises to see us through it.

Kids with cancer often spend a lot of time in hospitals. So I asked some of them this question: "What do you think is the worst thing about being in the hospital?"

They told me that little things get on your nerves more when you're sick. One boy said that the worst thing for him is when nurses come into his room and wake him up at all hours of the day and night!

Nurses have an important job to do. They have to keep a close check on their patients during the day—and during the night. When a person is trying to sleep that could be annoying. But let's think about this another way. Where would the patients be without the nurses who care for them?

Dr. Devo is proclaiming this as "Pray for Nurses and Doctors Day!" In your prayers today, thank God for all those who take care of the sick. Pray for medical missionaries in other countries too. If you know nurses or doctors, thank God for them personally. You might even want to send each of them a "thank you" note. Happy "Pray for Nurses and Doctors Day!" Pray that patients will be patient with their nurses today!

Is this verse appropriate for those who think the worst thing about being in the hospital is nurses who wake them up? "Pray for those who persecute you," (Matthew 5:44). As far as nurses are concerned, that should say, "Pray for those who protect you!"

Kids with Cancer
(Fifth of six)

I asked some of the kids with cancer this question: "What miracle have you seen?" One cancer patient at the children's hospital responded, "Me!" He knew he was a walking, breathing, living miracle from heaven, even though he was in the hospital and still battling cancer. Things had been much worse for him, and he had seen many miracles in his life and body. He knew he was a miracle.

Sometimes we think of a miracle only as something super-big, like a cancer patient being completely healed. But often God sends little miracles through medication, treatments, and surgeries—miracles like strength for breathing from our lungs, being able to eat the littlest bit without throwing it up, and just being alive for another day.

If you don't think you've seen a miracle, all you have to do is look into a mirror. You are a living, breathing miracle from heaven! God is working in your life every minute. His love and forgiveness are miracles. He is doing miracles for you, in you, around you, and through you every day. Check it out! Keep your eyes and ears open for them (by the way, your eyes and ears are miracles too)! Enjoy God's daily life-changing miracles. Thank him for the miracle in the mirror!

> He does wonderful things that can't be understood. He does miracles that can't even be counted.
>
> Job 5:9 NIRV

KIDS WITH CANCER
(SIXTH OF SIX)

Check out this awesome prayer written by Tyler, a patient at a children's hospital. I asked him to write a prayer about anything he'd like. This is what he wrote and prayed: "Dear God, please don't let my sister or brother get sick like me. Amen."

Wow! Tyler could have asked to be healed. He could have asked that the cancer treatments he was taking wouldn't make him sick. He could have prayed for a million things for himself, but instead, he chose to pray for his brother and sister. That's totally awesome! That's love!

There's nothing wrong with asking God for something for yourself. But it is also wonderful to think about the needs, concerns, and lives of others. When you see how God loves you in Jesus, it helps you to love others and be concerned for their lives and faith.

> If we love one another, God lives in us and his love is made complete in us.
>
> 1 JOHN 4:12

Tyler, you "wowed" D.J. and me with your answer! Even though you have cancer in your blood— leukemia—your heart is amazing!

LOL!
(Laughing Out Loud)

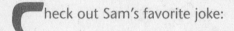

Check out Sam's favorite joke:

Q: What do you get when you cross a bridge with a pogo stick?

A: You get to the other side!

Get it? Do you get it? Huh? Do you? You get to the other side of the bridge. Sometimes answers are so obvious. After we hear them, we feel silly because we should have known. For instance, what's the answer to the question, "How can someone cross from earth into heaven?" For sure, it won't be on a pogo stick!

The answer is obvious. There is only one way to heaven and that is through faith (placing our trust) in Jesus Christ and what he has done for us. He died on the cross, taking our sin on himself. He took the punishment we deserved for our sins, and he gave us back forgiveness for all those sins. So many people have it all wrong. They think it's up to them to get themselves to heaven. The Bible makes it very clear! It's not about us! It's all about Jesus. The Holy Spirit even creates our faith in him, since we can't believe on our own.

Check out these true words from the Bible: "It is by grace you have been saved, through faith—and this not from yourselves, it is the gift of God—not by works, so that no one can boast." And "No one can say 'Jesus is Lord,' except by the Holy Spirit." It's obvious, isn't it? Thank you, Jesus!

Time for a Miracle
(First of Nine)

If you could ask Jesus to do one miracle for you right now, what would it be and why?

What miracle would you ask for? Go on—answer! How about asking Jesus to help your family get along better? Only a few kids actually mentioned that one. But we think that a lot of kids might be thinking about it.

Some of you reading this book need that very miracle. If that includes you, it may be a good time for you and your family to talk about things that will help you get along better. See if you can, as a group or by yourself, think of things that you can do for each other. At the bottom of the page is a prayer your family can pray together or you can pray by yourself.

No family gets along perfectly all the time. That's because we are all sinners. Perfect families are only in heaven. But there are things you may need to talk about so you can all be happier, with God's help. Love is patient and kind (1 Corinthians 13:4). Patience is when people don't expect each other to be perfect, and kind is when they forgive each other's imperfections.

Prayer:
Dear Jesus, the miracle-worker,
family friend, and Savior. It seems like sometimes
our family needs a miracle so we can get along
better. Give us wisdom to know how to do that.
Bring us peace. Lead us to forgive and love each other
like you love and forgive us. Thank you for your help
with this. I pray in your name. Amen.

21

TiME FOR A MiRACLE
(SECOND OF NiNE)

If you could ask Jesus to do one miracle for you right now, what would it be and why?

I think Jenny and Christopher would like to get out of some homework! Jenny said she would ask Jesus to make it summer all the time! And in the winter, Christopher said, he'd ask for a lot of snow, so school would be out!

Okay, whine about having to go to school. (Go ahead! Have a whining contest if you want!) Feel better? I didn't think you would! Hey, we all had to go to school. But school's for your good! Really!

> Let us learn together
> what is good.
> Job 34:4

Just think if you laid at the pool like it was summer all year round and never did anything else. Or imagine spending 365 days just playing in the snow. That might sound great now, but over the years you'd get sick from all the sun or frozen from too much snow!

And you wouldn't have learned anything! You wouldn't have used or developed the brains God gave you. You wouldn't be able to get a good job when you get older because you didn't learn about reading, speeling (make that 'spelling'), writing, science, math, art, or computers. Most importantly, you wouldn't have shared his good news with others in school.

Thank God for school! Thank him for summer vacations! Thank him for snow days (depending on where you live)! Thank him for brains, teachers, classmates, and Sunday schools too!

TiME FOR A MiRACLE
(THiRD OF NiNE)

If you could ask Jesus to do one miracle for you right now, what would it be and why?

One girl gave us a very interesting answer. She said, "I would ask him to take every bad thing I've ever done and throw it in the trash can."

That answer reminded me of the time I spent jetting around the world trying to create a machine that would totally destroy sins. I tried to make it with a newfangled shredder, a laser blaster, and an invisible paint that would wash them away. But nothing worked, so I gave up.

> As far as the east is from the west, so far has he removed our transgressions [sins] from us.
>
> PSALM 103:12

My assistant, D.J., is just pretty smart. He told me not to give up on finding help erasing all the bad things I had done. "But," he said, "the only way is to give up all your sins to Jesus." I had too many sins to fill a trash can, and they couldn't be zapped or shredded. But God forgives completely. D.J. showed me these verses in the Bible.

> Then he adds, "I will not remember their sins anymore. I will not remember the evil things they have done."
>
> HEBREWS 10:17 (NIRV)

To the girl who wanted Jesus to throw her bad things in the trash can—your prayers are answered! The miracle is done! Your sins aren't in a trash can but they are gone forever!

PRAYER PONDER POINT

Whose faith would you like to pray for? One boy had some special people on his heart. This is his prayer: "Dear God, please help my family believe in you more and come to church more often so they will know that they are saved because they trust and follow you. Amen."

That boy's prayer has so much concern and love packed into one sentence. Maybe you aren't sure that some of your relatives believe in Jesus, and you want to pray for them today.

Here are some prayer points to ponder:

• Pray that the Holy Spirit would help you be an example to your relatives who don't know Jesus.

• Pray that the Holy Spirit would give you words to share with them.

• Pray that God will send other people into their lives to share Jesus' saving news with them.

Jesus told his disciples a parable to show them that they should always pray and not give up.

LUKE 18:1

• Pray that those relatives would find a church where God's Word is taught.

• Pray that you would never give up praying for them.

BiBLE VERSE
FiLL-iN-THE-_____!

The Lord will quiet you with his _____; he will rejoice over you with _____.

Which of the following answers for the blanks do you think is right?

(A) He will quiet you with his power; he will rejoice over you with love. (Ian)

(B) He will quiet you with his hand; he will rejoice over you with angels. (Ben)

(C) He will quiet you with his voice; he will rejoice over you with a song. (Alicia)

(D) He will quiet you with his hand; he will rejoice over you with fireworks. (James)

(E) He will quiet you with his love; he will rejoice over you with singing. (Zephaniah)

These all are good answers. The Lord could quiet us with his power, love, hand, or voice. And to think of the Lord rejoicing over us in any way is incredible! Fireworks in heaven! Angels rejoicing with him! God sharing good news with us! But Zephaniah has the answer from the Bible—that's because it's written in his Old Testament book.

Try to memorize Zephaniah 3:17. What do the words mean to you? Pray something like:

Thank you,
Lord, for quieting me with your
love when I am upset, scared, or nervous. It
doesn't seem possible that you would rejoice over me
with singing! I am so honored! I want to sing your
praises and share your love forever!
Amen.

LOL!
(LAUGHING OUT LOUD)

Christine shared this joke with D.J. and me:

Q: What did Jesus say when Peter, his disciple, asked him how he wanted his steak cooked?

A: Well done, good and faithful servant!

If you don't get the joke, you might want to read the parable in Matthew 25:14–29. It tells about a man who gives his servants a certain amount of money before leaving on a trip. When he returns, the master wants to know what each servant did with the money he had been given. Two of the servants doubled the money. But a third one was afraid he might lose it, so he buried it in the ground!

To the two servants who wisely used the gifts from their master, he said, "Well done, good and faithful servant." But he thought the last servant wasted what he had been given by not using it to make more. He wasn't happy with that servant.

Jesus told this parable to remind his followers to use their gifts wisely. What gifts has God given you? How do you use those gifts to give him glory? Won't it be wonderful to hear Jesus say to us, "Well done, good and faithful servant"?

THAT'S WEIRD!

What's the weirdest creature God created?

Some really unique, different—okay, just weird creatures are out there! Some have weird names, and others do strange things.

Rick thinks the dung beetle is pretty weird because of its name. Kyle says to just look at the hippo—it's weird! And Amanda thinks the puffer fish is pretty strange. It blows itself up! Those *are* some *odd* creatures!

As my ship takes me flying all over the land sharing devotions with kids, I'm seeing some weird creatures. But I remember that God created all his creatures with a purpose and made them in very unique ways to live safely in the places he put them. And I also have to remember that when God saw all he created (yes, even the dung beetles, the hip-popotamuses, and the puffer fish), he reviewed his creation and declared it to be good (Genesis 1:31).

Okay, okay, God. I get the picture. All you create is good and has a purpose, but I still think spiders and snakes are creepy!

Thank you, Lord, for all your incredible creation!

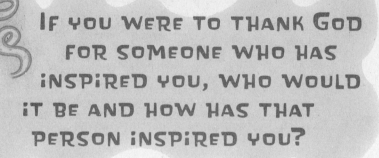

IF YOU WERE TO THANK GOD FOR SOMEONE WHO HAS INSPIRED YOU, WHO WOULD IT BE AND HOW HAS THAT PERSON INSPIRED YOU?

Interviewing kids with this question brought lots of smiles. One young girl said, "Lauren inspired me by being so nice." Three cheers for Lauren's gift of kindness! See how simple inspiring someone can be?

Meghan wanted to tell us that Emilie is an inspiration because "she taught me to listen to the people who are talking about Jesus." Let's give Emilie a standing ovation! You inspire us all, Emilie! Keep teaching others to listen to those who are talking about Jesus. And keep sharing your loving heart!

One sweet girl decided her mom has inspired her. Then she added, "But don't tell her!" I don't agree! When people inspire you, you should tell them. Let your mom know how much you appreciate her! You'll be glad you did!

The apostles Paul, Silas, and Timothy said they could see how God's people living in the city of Thessalonica were inspired by hope in Jesus Christ. (You can read about it in 1 Thessalonians 1:2–3.) Jesus is the best inspiration. He inspires us to be hopeful even when things seem hopeless. You are our inspiration, Jesus. Help us to encourage and inspire others with your hope.

WHAT DO YOU THINK IS JESUS' FAVORITE MIRACLE?

Correna wrote: That I love him!

That is a miracle, isn't it? It's a miracle that we love Jesus! It's also a miracle that he would love us. No matter how many special things D.J. and I mix up in our lab, we couldn't make something that would cause us to love Jesus. But God did a miracle by placing faith in our hearts.

Are you still scratching your head wondering why it's a miracle that we love Jesus? Here's the scoop. First of all, we weren't born with faith. In fact, the Bible tells us that when it comes to faith, we couldn't do anything ourselves to believe in Jesus. (If you want to study this further, read Ephesians 2:1, 1 Corinthians 2:14, and Romans 8:7.) We have no power of our own to come to Jesus. The Holy Spirit has called us by name and placed faith in us through his Word. What a miracle!

Yes, Correna, it's a great miracle that any of us believe in him! Thank God for the miracle of your growing, saving faith right now!

WHAT'S YOUR LEAST FAVORITE THING ABOUT GOING TO CHURCH?

This interview question received some interesting answers like:

- Standing up so long. (Amy)

- Sitting in the hard wooden pews. (Matthew)

- A very long sermon. (Steven)

- When I can't find my spot in the hymnal. (Katherine)

My least favorite thing about going to church is the temptation to think about those things—things that make me selfishly uncomfortable. The devil loves to distract me from receiving what God wants to give me during a service. These distractions also keep me from fully giving God the kind of worship he deserves. And that's what the devil loves! He wants me to think about myself instead of Jesus Christ! What a sneaky trick to use right in the middle of a worship service.

> May the words of my mouth and the thoughts of my heart be pleasing in your eyes, you are my Rock and my Redeemer.
>
> PSALM 19:14 (NIRV)

One way God can help you take your mind off yourself and focus on him is for you to pray before, during, and after the church service. Ask God to send his angels to keep the devil and his temptations away. Ask him to open your heart and mind so you can concentrate on what he has to say and worship God with all your heart. Ask him to keep praise in your heart every day of the week—not just on Sundays!

BIBLE VERSE
FILL-IN-THE-_____!

The fruit of the Spirit is _____.

D.J. and I got lots of different answers for this interview question. Some were:

A song of praise . . . love . . . faith . . . in you . . . joyful words . . . self-control . . . hope. We also got four votes for an apple, two for grapes, and two for an orange!

A couple of those were correct, according to Galatians 5:22–23, which reads, "The fruit of the Spirit is love, joy, peace, patience, kindness, goodness, faithfulness, gentleness and self-control."

What does "the fruit of the Spirit" mean? Let's put it this way. If you plant an apple tree in the ground, what would you expect to find growing on it? Apples or pears? Do grapes grow on a plum tree? If you are planted in God's Word, called to be a Christian—a follower of Jesus Christ who has the Holy Spirit living in you—what kind of fruit should you be producing?

The Bible says that fruit should be love, joy, peace, patience, kindness, goodness, faithfulness, gentleness, and self-control. Can you remember all nine? Try it without looking at this page. Are you bearing fruit like that? If so, you can thank the Spirit who is living in you! Go and keep growing, bearing fruit that will last!

LOL!
(Laughing Out Loud)

Daniel, from Texas, told me his favorite joke.

> Knock-knock!
>
> Who's there?
>
> Cuckoo.
>
> Cuckoo who?
>
> Cuckoo yourself—I didn't come here to be insulted!

Insults aren't nice. When you insult someone, you are making fun of that person, and you are also making fun of God who created him or her!

No one likes to be insulted. But there is a time when Jesus says you can be happy when you are insulted. Here's what Jesus said, "Blessed are you when people insult you . . . because of me" (Matthew 5:11). What do you think is the difference between this verse and just being made fun of by someone? It's the last three words. Jesus said, "Blessed are you when people insult you . . . because of me."

Jesus knows no insults are fun. But sometimes when you stand up for Jesus, people will insult you. When those times come, know you are blessed. Let people know you love Jesus! Then know that God will bless you, no matter what other people do.

WHO'S THE MEANEST PERSON IN THE BIBLE?
(FIRST OF TWO)

We got lots of different answers for this question because of all the mean people in the Bible. Lots of mean people are living today too. Things haven't changed much, have they?

- Kate, Lauren, and others thought Judas was the meanest because he betrayed Jesus. (Read Luke 22:3–6.)

- Nick, Erik, Kelsey, and Miles voted for King Herod because he tried to kill Jesus. (Read Matthew 2:13–16.)

- Brian and Sarah thought Cain was the mean person of the Bible because he killed his own brother. (Read Genesis 4:3–16)

- The one who received the most votes for being mean was (someone give a drum roll please) . . . Satan!

Do you know that if it wasn't for the devil—Mr. Mean himself—Judas wouldn't have betrayed Jesus, King Herod wouldn't have tried to kill Jesus, and Cain wouldn't have killed his brother. If the world was perfect, there would be no sin, no betrayal, no death, no evil, no one being mean. Because of sin, there will be mean people and even we will do mean things.

But we can't just blame Satan. He doesn't force us to do mean things. We choose to follow his temptations! Thankfully, Jesus keeps calling us to follow him and his forgiving ways. That truth means a lot for people who live in a mean world!

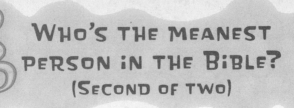

WHO'S THE MEANEST PERSON IN THE BIBLE?
(SECOND OF TWO)

Becca and Nick also gave good answers to this question we discussed in yesterday's devotion. They said Saul was the meanest person because he killed Christians. The story of Saul—who you may know better as Paul the Apostle, one of the greatest missionaries for Christ—is one of the greatest stories in the Bible.

Becca and Nick were right. Saul was a religious man who hated Christians, and he was responsible for many of them being arrested and killed. But then Jesus changed his life. And what a change it was! Paul went from being one of the meanest people around to loving Jesus and spreading his word to the entire world. There's a great lesson here for us to remember.

Can you think of some people who are mean or have done horrible things? I'm guessing you've thought they can't change. If you ever think that, remember Saul/Paul. The people who knew him couldn't believe he had totally changed. But the real secret is that he didn't change himself—God changed him. And he is still changing people today! Read this powerful story of God changing Paul's life from mean to meaningful in Acts 9:1–31.

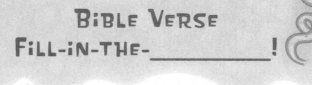

Bible Verse
Fill-in-the-_____!

Praise the Lord. Praise him with _____.

It's great to praise the Lord! And there are so many ways to praise him. This is how some of the kids filled in the blank:

(A) Praise him with smiles!

(B) Praise him with glory and grace!

(C) Praise him with joy!

(D) Praise him with cymbals, tambourines, and dance!

(E) Praise him with prayer and song!

(F) Praise him with all your heart, soul, and mind!

(G) Praise him with joyful songs!

(H) Praise him with thanks!

(I) Praise him with love, music, and joy!

Those are great ways to praise the Lord! Psalm 150 says, "Praise the Lord. . . . Praise him with the sounding of the trumpet, praise him with the harp and lyre, praise him with tambourine and dancing, praise him the strings and flute, praise him with the clash of cymbals, praise him with resounding cymbals. Let everything that has breath praise the Lord. Praise the Lord." I know you have breath. So how will you praise the Lord today?

TiME FOR A MiRACLE
(FOURTH OF NiNE)

If you could ask Jesus to do one miracle for you right now, what would it be and why?

We had to smile when we heard this answer to the miracle question. A ten-year-old said, "Change my sister to a boy!" I have a feeling the person must have had a family fight just before answering that question! Or maybe this is a boy who has an older sister—the only clothes he gets are hand-me-downs, and he is tired of wearing his sister's clothes!

Sometimes it's hard for brothers and sisters to get along. It's tough because brothers and sisters live close together in the same house. That means they're going to bug each other sometimes.

Do you have a brother or sister who gets on your nerves? If so, do you think you ever get on his or her nerves? Lots of kids don't have brothers and sisters but would love to have some. They might remind you that it's a blessing to have other kids in your family.

When you get upset at your brother or sister (or other family members), take time out and pray about that. It's hard to stay mad when you're praying!

David wrote, "How good and pleasant it is when brothers live together in unity!" (Psalm 133:1). Let's add two words to that: "How good and pleasant it is when brothers [and sisters] live together in unity!"

Time for a Miracle?
(Fifth of Nine)

If you could ask Jesus to do one miracle for you right now, what would it be and why?

In one classroom I visited to interview kids, the students have a classmate and friend, Becky, who has been sick a lot. She needs two new lungs. The class said that's the miracle they want—for Becky to get the double lung transplant she needs and be healed.

The gift of healing for someone who is sick is a great miracle to ask for. It's great to see friends and classmates who care about each other. The Bible says we are all part of one body—the Body of Christ. We are all important.

In talking about the Body of Christ, Paul writes to the believers in the city of Corinth saying, "God has joined together all the parts of the body. . . . All of them will take care of each other. If one part suffers, every part suffers with it. If one part is honored, every part shares in its joy" (1 Corinthians 12:25–26 NIrV).

Who are you hurting with today? Who are you rejoicing with?

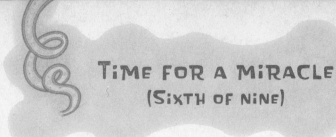

If you could ask Jesus to do one miracle for you right now, what would it be and why?

Kurt's answer to that question cracked me up. "Let me find a hundred bucks!" Hey Kurt, you had your chance. You could have asked for a thousand bucks or maybe a million! But you only asked for a hundred? Maybe you've been learning about having to pay taxes in school and thought a hundred bucks would be best.

Or maybe Kurt likes to hunt deer and was asking to find a hundred bucks (male deer)! A hundred deer would be more than enough. You couldn't find a home freezer big enough for that much deer meat!

Sometimes we think too small. We don't think God really wants to bless us in big ways. Take time now to read Paul's prayer found in Ephesians 3:16–21. Pray it out loud. Then, think about the words in verse 20: "Now to him who is able to do immeasurably more than all we ask or imagine ... " Imagine what plans God has for you!

By the way, happy hunting, Kurt—for money or deer!

TiME FOR A MiRACLE
(SEVENTH OF NiNE)

If you could ask Jesus to do one miracle for you right now, what would it be and why?

Which of these miracles would you choose?

(A) Make me an excellent chef. (Nick)

(B) Make everyone green blobs just because it would be cool. (Adoria)

(C) Give me lots of video games so I would never be bored. (Steven)

(D) Make all the wars end. (Mallorie)

(E) Stop world hunger. (Kayla)

That's a hard one, isn't it? (Well, maybe not the green-blob answer!) Some are about individuals and some about miracles for our world. Some are very serious, while others are fun.

Those answers remind us that we can talk to God about anything that's important to us—everything from world peace to not being bored. Whatever is important to us is important to him! That's great news from our great Savior!

What miracle prayer do you have in mind to talk to him about?

TiME FOR A MiRACLE
(EiGHTH OF NiNE)

If you could ask Jesus to do one miracle for you right now, what would it be and why?

Deborah has a fantastic miracle request for Jesus—that more people will learn about him so more people will go to heaven. You have a great heart for Jesus and his purpose on this earth, Deborah. And it sounds like you know your purpose in life—spreading the good news about Jesus.

Did you know that's one of your purposes in life too? It is! Everyone has a purpose. Even dolphins have a porpoise in life! (That's a joke, in case you didn't notice!)

One of our purposes is to share the saving news of Jesus Christ—making sure people know Jesus is the only way to heaven and that he wants to spend eternity with them! When Paul wrote about sharing the news of heaven with others, he wrote, "God has made us for that very purpose. He has given us the Holy Spirit as a down payment. The Spirit makes us sure of what is still to come" (2 Corinthians 5:5 NIrV).

The miracle of making sure that people know Jesus as their personal Lord and Savior can happen through you and me! What a miracle! What good news!

If you could ask Jesus to do one miracle for you right now, what would it be and why?

Many kids said they would ask that their relatives who had died—grandmas and grandpas, aunts and uncles, and others—would be brought back to life.

When someone dies, we miss them very much. We feel very sad inside. It's okay to feel that way. It's normal to cry.

At times, almost everybody wishes someone special who has died could come back to life. But there's another side to the story. If our relatives died believing in Jesus as their Savior, we know they're in heaven. They are perfectly happy and loved. Their souls are with Jesus.

When you realize those who died having faith in Jesus are in a perfect place, you will probably feel happy for them. And even though you'll still miss them, you may start looking forward to the day we will all be together again in heaven. That day will come, you know. The Bible says that all followers of Jesus Christ will spend eternity together in heaven with God.

In telling us about heaven, John wrote, "[Jesus] will wipe away every tear from their eyes. There will be no more death or mourning or crying or pain, . . . I am making everything new!" (Revelation 21:4–5).

41

WHAT WAS THE EASIEST ANIMAL FOR ADAM TO NAME?

Derek thinks the easiest to name was the dog because they just spelled God backward! Lee thought it would be the fly. Why? Because it flies!

Good thinking, guys! Of course, if Lee had named the animals, then fish would be called "swims," cows and deer would be called "walks," and snakes would be called "slides"—but I still like his creative thinking!

Ask those around you. Do they think naming the animals would be easy, hard, fun, or boring? Here were God's instructions according to Genesis 2:19: "Now the Lord God had formed out of the ground all the beasts of the field and all the birds of the air. He brought them to the man to see what he would name them; and whatever the man called each living creature, that was its name."

That was a big job! So many animals and birds needed names. It's a fun mind picture, imagining God bringing the animals and birds to Adam for him to name. You could have fun making up a skit with one person being Adam (who'd make up names) and others pretending to be different animals and birds.

God gives us each special things to do. Next time you have a big project, think of God himself bringing it to you, working beside you, and having fun with it!

WHY DO YOU THINK DANIEL CHOSE TO EAT VEGETABLES INSTEAD OF THE KING'S DELICIOUS FOOD?

Which answer (or answers) given by our kid experts, do you think is (are) correct?

(A) Because who needs good, delicious food when you have vegetables! (John)

(B) He wanted to be healthy. (Mike)

(C) Because the king's food was probably sacrificed to a different god. (Alexia)

This story is found in Daniel 1. You might want to read it before reading the correct answer below. Daniel was a child of God. He loved God and was determined to follow him. King Nebuchadnezzar wanted Daniel and others to eat his choice foods. But Daniel knew the king's food had first been offered to idols. Daniel and his three friends wanted no part of that. Even though he knew the king's idols weren't real, he didn't want anything to do with that.

We might think some things we take part in aren't a big deal. But if they go against God's will, then we should have nothing to do with them. That can be tough. God blessed those who stood up for his ways. Daniel 1:17 says, "To these four young men God gave knowledge and understanding of all kinds of literature and learning. And Daniel could understand visions and dreams of all kinds."

Although all the moms I talked to thought John and Mike were correct, Alexia had the right idea!

LOL!
(Laughing Out Loud)

A man is eating at a restaurant. He says, "Hey waiter, this soup tastes funny."

The waiter asks, "Then why aren't you laughing?"

Isn't it great to laugh? Laughing is a great gift from God! If you're reading this with others, take turns trying to make each other laugh without touching. Is it easy? Wouldn't it be sad if God hadn't created laughter? (That's kind of a dumb question, isn't it?)

This day is sacred to our Lord. Do not grieve, for the joy of the Lord is your strength.

Nehemiah 8:10b

Just spend a minute or two thinking about or sharing true stories or favorite jokes—and laugh, laugh, laugh! Who do you think has the best laugh? Who has God blessed with a great smile that makes other people smile? Thank God for the gift of laughter and joy. Thank him that through his promises that bring us joy—even on really bad days—he gives us extra strength to make it through each and every day.

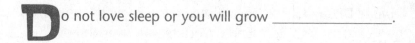

BIBLE VERSE
FILL-IN-THE-_____!

Do not love sleep or you will grow _____.

Hey, what's up with these words? Doesn't every kid love to sleep? Well, not every one! This is a warning from the book of Proverbs about loving sleep too much. My lab computer reported some interesting answers to this fill-in-the-blank.

Which do you think is right? "Do not love sleep or you will grow—

> (A) very, very, very tall   (E) weak
>
> (B) to hate day   (F) healthy
>
> (C) lazy   (G) poor
>
> (D) tired all the time   (H) none of the above

I would tell you the answer now, but (yawn) it's time for my nap. While I'm napping in my rocket-shaped bed, you can look up the answer in your Bible. Read Proverbs 20:13. Then think about why you think the wise writer of these words wrote them.

I'll be (yawn) back sometime (stretch) later. I'm starting to fade off to slee—"

WERE THE DISCIPLES PERFECT?

Everyone D.J. and I interviewed seemed to know the answer to this question. It's "No!" God's Word tells us over and over that everyone—except Jesus—sinned. One place it tells us this is in Romans 3:23, "All have sinned and fall short of the glory of God." Hebrews 4:15 reminds us that Jesus was "tempted in every way, just as we are—yet was without sin."

The Bible gives a lot of examples of the disciples sinning. Can you think of any? They were not perfect at all. Now think about the sins you have committed as a disciple (a follower) of Jesus. That's not fun to do!

Aren't you glad the disciples' stories (and our story) don't end with the sin? The sin ends up at the cross with Jesus. The Bible says: "Christ didn't have any sin. But God made him become sin for us. So that we can be made right with God because of what Christ has done for us" (2 Corinthians 5:21 NIrv). That's a story with a happy ending for disciples all over the world!

By the way, if you want to see a list of the disciples, check out Luke 6:13–16. (For Dr. Devo extra credit—like that's worth anything—find the name of the disciple who took the place of Judas in Acts 1:21–26.)

WHAT ARE THE TWO BOOKS OF THE BIBLE NAMED AFTER WOMEN?

My interview microphone picked up these guesses:

(A) Ephesians

(E) Obadiah

(B) Jude

(F) Corinthians

(C) Nehemiah

(G) Galatians

(D) Habakkuk

The correct answer is: Esther and Ruth! If you've never read these books in the Bible, I hope you will! Both are written as stories about the women they're named for. The book of Ruth is only four chapters long. Ruth wasn't from Israel, but God brought her into his family. The book about her is a reminder that God's salvation is for all people.

Dr. Devo Trivia Alert! Esther is the only book in the Bible that doesn't have the name God in it! But the story is all about the special plan God had for Esther and his people.

God put us on earth at this time for a special purpose. Esther was elevated to her royal position for a very specific purpose—to save her people (Esther 4:14). God loves to work in the lives of all people. Everyone is important to him—women, men, boys, and girls of all ages, colors, and countries.

If God were to write a story about your life, what would some of the chapters be called? In what ways would he say he has worked in your life? What do you think the title of the book should be? You know what? God is writing his story and your story as you live every day!

WHAT WiLL HEAVEN LOOK LiKE?

I think most kids (and adults) try to picture in their minds what heaven will look like. In fact, the most popular answer kids your age give is that in heaven everything will be white. Lydia went a different direction and said she had it pictured as a great big yellow place. And James threw in a great thought. He reported that he thinks heaven will look like God! Good answer, bro!

Revelation 21:22–23 tells us there will be no need for the sun or moon in heaven because the glory of God gives it light and the Lamb (Jesus) is its lamp.

We don't know all the details about heaven. When God created his perfect paradise the first time (The Garden of Eden) it was filled with green trees and bushes and rivers. God has an eternity to show us every beautiful part of his heaven. What an honor to live with him!

(By the way, in case you're wondering what my Dr. Devo laboratory looks like . . . well . . . in a weird kind of way, it's similar to the answers about heaven. It has yellow walls and lots of white, as well as orange, green, and lots of other wild, colorful things. It doesn't look like God though. It looks like me—a mess!)

IS IT A SIN TO GET ANGRY?

The answers to this Dr. Devo question were pretty much split between "yes" and "no." But some kids wrote comments like:

(A) Not always. (Willie)

(B) Sometimes. (Lauren)

(C) Not exactly. (Meghan)

Willie, Lauren, and Meghan hit the bull's-eye, along with those who said, "no." Anger is an emotion God has created so we can deal with tough times. But it can easily become a sin when we use it in a hurtful way. It's how we handle our anger that makes the difference.

That's why Paul wrote, "In your anger do not sin" (Ephesians 4:26). He warns us to stay away from rage and anger because they can so easily turn into sinful actions.

Think about ways of dealing with anger that are not sinful. What are some sinful ways people deal with anger? When do you have trouble with anger? Close with a prayer, asking God to help you and those around you handle anger in a way that pleases him.

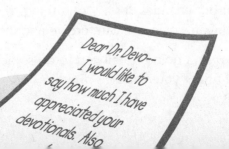

Dear Dr. Devo—
I would like to say how much I have appreciated your devotionals. Also

Biff Tonberg
101 Mother St.
Greenburg, SC 10609

Dr. Devo

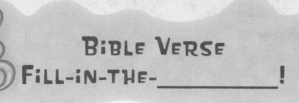

BIBLE VERSE
FiLL-iN-THE-_____!

Pray for those who _____ you.

Almost any answer would fit in the blank, wouldn't it? Pray for those who—

(A) eat ice cream with

(B) buy Dr. Devo devotion books for

(C) smile at

The possibilities are endless! Some of the answers kids gave us include:

(A) hate   (E) persecute

(B) hurt   (F) thank

(C) are needier than   (G) protect

(D) love   (H) harm

Those all work! We are to pray for everyone! If we want to quote Matthew 5:44, then the correct answer is "persecute." To persecute others means to hurt them. Often it means to continue to hurt them in a mean way.

Wait a minute! It's easy to pray for someone who eats ice cream with you or protects you or smiles at you. But if someone hurts you, you're supposed to pray for them? That's hard. Jesus said we are to pray for our enemies. It's a tough thing to do, but it we find that, with God's help, we can forgive and control our anger.

You know Jesus isn't going to tell you to do something that's not good for you! Aren't you glad he's on your side?

50

WHAT IS A PROVERB?

Alex gets the Creative Thinking Award for his answer: "It's a sentence with a lot of verbs in it—PRO*VERBS*. What do you think about these answers?

(A) A book in the Bible. (Paul)

(B) Short parables. (Willie)

(C) A really encouraging story. (Sunni)

(D) An ancient saying. (Erik)

(E) A very smart saying. (Becca)

(F) It describes how you should treat other people and things. (Miranda)

(G) A word of wisdom. (Christiana)

Great answers, friends! They are all right in their own way. Proverbs is a book in the Bible. In a way, you could call proverbs short parables in that they teach us lessons. The proverbs in the Bible encourage us to live in God's ways. Many are ancient and very smart sayings. Often they describe how you should treat people and things. But Christina sums it up best: Proverbs are words of wisdom.

Solomon wrote many of the Bible's proverbs. God gave him great wisdom. Most of the wise sayings in the book of Proverbs are only one verse long. Check them out in your Bible now, while I leave you with this one: "If you really want to gain knowledge, you must begin by having respect for the Lord. But foolish people hate wisdom and training" (Proverbs 1:7 NIrv).

PRAYER
PONDER POINT

**Do you pray for your Pastor very often?
Why or why not?**

Most kids answered with something like, "Not really, because I don't think about it very often." Well, let's get that changed!

Not all ministers are called a "pastor," but the word means "shepherd." A pastor is called to be a shepherd to the flock of God's people in a certain area. Pastors need many, many prayers! Add the ideas below for your pastor to your prayer list. Pray for:

(A) A strong faith—joy in serving—good health.

(B) Wisdom in making decisions and helping people.

(C) Dealing with temptations—the right words to say.

(D) Family—friendships—the church staff.

(E) Creativity in writing sermons–a love for God's people.

(F) Humility—extra time to laugh and have fun.

(G) A love for those who don't know Jesus.

(H) Lots of help in carrying out God's plan for the church.

WHAT IS SOMETHING
YOU DID THAT PROBABLY
MADE JESUS LAUGH?
(ONE OF TWO)

Check out these funny moments kids shared:

- (A) Aaron shot an air ball at a basketball game.

- (B) Audra fell in the mud.

- (C) Riley thought Jesus laughed when he was learning to walk.

- (D) Caitlyn put the ham in the microwave instead of the refrigerator.

- (E) Lindsey rode her bike into her pond.

It's easy to feel silly when we do goofy things! But you can be certain that our God will never laugh at us! Now he may laugh with us, but not at us! I'm sure some of my goof-ups and silliness could cause the most serious of angels to break a smile!

It's too bad we often picture Jesus as a sad, serious, dull Savior. How could he not smile watching the eyes of a blind man light up after healing him? Don't you think seeing a newly healed lame man skip down the street would cause him to laugh with joy?

Isaiah 62:5 says, "As a bridegroom rejoices over his bride, so will your God rejoice over you!" You've probably seen couples who are getting married nearly bursting with joy over each other. Guess what? Jesus loves you more than that! He's so happy about your life with him that he's rejoicing over you right now! Smile and say . . . Jeeeeesus!

WHAT IS SOMETHING YOU DID THAT PROBABLY MADE JESUS LAUGH?
(SECOND OF TWO)

Several kids answered that question by saying, "I told a joke." There's nothing like a good joke and a fun laugh to follow! D.J. and I love telling each other jokes between devotion experiments!

Jokes are good fun—if they are the right kind of jokes. There are plenty of not-so-good jokes out there, though—jokes that God would want us to stay away from. Some of those jokes make fun of people. Those aren't cool. Others are called dirty jokes because they make fun of the bodies God created for us or other gifts he meant to be special. Some jokes use bad words or cause people to laugh at things God wouldn't want them to laugh at. Not all jokes are the kind God would want us to tell.

When you're tempted to tell a bad joke or say something that wouldn't be a blessing to God, you can pray the words of Psalm 141:3. It says, "Set a guard over my mouth, O Lord; keep watch over the door of my lips."

Okay, before you have a prayer about guarding your mouth, how about a joke?

> Q: Was there any money on Noah's ark?
>
> A: The ducks had a couple bills, and the skunks put in their two scents!

IF YOU COULD ASK MARY A QUESTION, WHAT WOULD IT BE?

Rosalie had a powerful question for the mother of Jesus. If she could, she'd ask Mary, "How did you feel when Jesus was on the cross dying?" Obviously, I can't answer that question. I'm not Mary. I wasn't there. And I'm not a mother. I've never seen death by crucifixion.

If you would like some idea of what a mother would feel, you might want to ask your mother, stepmother, or grandmother. I can tell you this much. Mary loved her son, Jesus, with all her heart. Probably no words can describe how awful she felt.

As difficult as it was for Mary, she was a woman of great faith. Think about what she said and did when an angel told her she would be the mother of the Savior of the world! As she stood by the cross, she may have remembered the words the angel had told her more than thirty years before, "Nothing is impossible with God" (Luke 1:37).

On Friday, Mary watched her son die. On Sunday, the impossible happened. She saw him alive! He had risen! Nothing is impossible with God!

LOL!
(Laughing Out Loud)

Geography teacher: What shape is the world in?

Student: Rotten!

Have you heard people say that the world is in rotten shape? They feel like the world is filled with bad news and there's no good news anywhere. Things are rotten in Denmark, the United States, China, Africa, Russia, Germany—it's rotten all over! That's because there's sin all over the world!

But it's not all bad news because Jesus has won a mighty victory over sin! Maybe people don't see much good news on television or in newspapers, but if they read the Bible, they know there is hope and help for a rotten, sinful world!

Read these encouraging words from Hebrews 12:3: "Consider [Jesus] who endured such opposition from sinful men, so that you will not grow weary and lose heart." Jesus lived in rotten times and a sinful world, too. But he made it through the rotten times for us. He brought us hope. He doesn't want us to give up! He's here to help and there's nothing rotten in that news!

WHY DON'T PEOPLE IN THE BIBLE HAVE LAST NAMES? AND IF YOU WERE TO GIVE JESUS A LAST NAME, WHAT WOULD IT BE AND WHY?

Here are a few answers D.J. and I received for these questions:

(A) I don't know why they didn't have last names. I would give Jesus the last name "Crider" because that's my last name. Hmmmm. Jesus Crider. What do you think? (Nick)

(B) They don't need them. I would give Jesus the last name "Heaven" because that's where he lives. (Chris)

(C) Last names weren't invented. I would give Jesus the last name "Holyman." (Liz)

Chris was right on when he noted people didn't need last names. They hadn't even been "invented" yet! At that time, the world didn't have as many people as it does now. Sometimes people were known by their father's name—for instance, James and John, sons of Zebedee, were two of Jesus' disciples.

That's your "Name Game" lesson for the day. Well, that's most of it. The rest includes memorizing and rejoicing in these words about the name of Jesus.

God exalted him to the highest place and gave him the name that is above every name, that at the name of Jesus every knee should bow, in heaven and on earth and under the earth.

PHILIPPIANS 2:9–10

BIBLE VERSE
FiLL-iN-THE-_____!

Your word is a _____ to my feet and a _____ to my path.

These are great words from Psalm 119:105.

Do you know the correct answers?

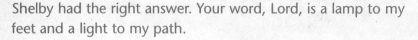

    (A) way; way (Miles)

    (B) lamp; light (Shelby)

    (C) rock; light (Mike and Alex)

    (D) road; lamp (Shawn)

Shelby had the right answer. Your word, Lord, is a lamp to my feet and a light to my path.

D.J. and I had some fun experimenting with this. We went out last night on a dark road. Since D.J. is small, he held a lamp by my feet as I walked. I was able to see in front of my feet so I wouldn't trip. It was great. Then I held a large light over my head and shined it down the street so I could see what was way ahead of me. Both lights were important.

God's Word is like a lamp and a bigger light. God's promises help guide us in every step we take. But they also help us see down the road. We don't know what will happen in the future, but the Word shows us that God's help will go ahead of us. It helps us make decisions about the future. It even shows us heaven, which is our real home, down the road.

I hope that sheds some light on the subject! Happy living in the light of God's Word!

WHAT QUESTION WOULD YOU LIKE TO ASK JESUS?
(FIRST OF FIFTEEN)

Am I going to heaven?

Do you think a lot of kids reading this devotion wonder the same thing? Many kids asked this when I interviewed them. They wanted to know for sure. Don't you? Why sit around worrying about it? There's actually a pretty easy way to find out. All you have to do is be totally honest in answering this question. Here it goes:

Do you believe that Jesus Christ, true God and true man, died on the cross and rose again so that he could be your personal Savior if you believe and trust in him?

As long as you can answer "yes" to that question, you are saved and going to heaven. Remember what John 3:16 says. In fact, let's make it personal. Put your name in the blanks. Ready?

"God so loved _____ that he gave his one and only Son, that [if] _____ believes in him _____ shall not perish but have eternal life."

Those are Jesus' own words. Heaven is open for you and all who believe in him as Savior. What a gift of love!

LicKETY SPLIT
Experimental
CLEAN-UP
Vacuum
5000

What came first, the chicken or the egg?

Very cute, Shanea! People have been asking that for years and arguing about the answer!

Personally, this Doctor of Devotions believes the chicken came first. Why? Because when God created the world, the Bible said he created the animals. It doesn't mention anything about starting with eggs! But that's just my opinion, Shanea!

Wait a minute. I do know there was a chicken in the Garden of Eden. I'm positive about that. In fact, there were two chickens. I even know their names! They were named Adam and Eve! They were "chicken" to obey God. Instead, they listened to this "bad egg" named Satan who tempted them to sin. After the two chickens did sin, biting into the fruit God told them not to eat, they tried to hide from God. What chickens! They went from being good eggs to being bad eggs because of sin. From then on, they were cooped up in a house of sin. Everything changed.

Thankfully, the yoke was on that bad egg Satan. In the end, God wins. How? He wins by sending a Savior from sin—his own perfect Son, Jesus. Three cheers for Jesus who wasn't too chicken to go to the cross for us!

WHAT QUESTION WOULD YOU LIKE TO ASK JESUS?
(THIRD OF FIFTEEN)

Will my parents get back together?

That is a question from the heart that a number of preteens said they would like to ask Jesus. When parents separate or get divorced, it's hard on the kids. It's hard on everyone. It's even hard for Jesus to watch. He doesn't like to see his children hurting.

While Jesus knows the answer to the question, "Will my parents get back together?" no one else knows. I hope these suggestions will help:

1. Ask your parents this question. Tell them your fears and concerns.

2. Ask your parents to pray for you and with you; tell them you'll pray for them.

3. Know that your parents love you even if they are having problems. Also know that God's love for you will never change, no matter what changes you go through.

4. Tell your parents you love them, even if you may not understand.

5. Talk to an adult or a friend you can trust (besides your parents) about your feelings.

6. Hold on to this promise God gave to Joshua and that he shares with you: "The Lord himself goes before you and will be with you; he will never leave you nor forsake you" (Deuteronomy 31:8).

When will Judgment Day be?

Hey Ashley, I know what Jesus will tell you when you ask! He will say he can't tell you. That's what he told his disciples too. He said, "No one knows about that day or hour, not even the angels in heaven, nor the Son, but only the Father" (Matthew 24:36). It's going to surprise everyone. If you ever hear someone say they know when Jesus is going to return, they're lying. No one knows.

I don't think that's the answer Ashley was hoping for. But since we don't know when Jesus will return, we need to be prepared at all times.

We prepare for a lot of things. We don't go to the store everyday to get just enough food for each meal. Teachers are glad we prepare for school. I've prepared for an emergency by keeping back-up jet fuel handy! But most importantly, we need to be prepared for Christ's return. We need to allow the Holy Spirit to keep our faith growing by staying close to God and his Word. Jesus has also told us to help others be prepared by telling them about his saving love.

Let's be prepared together, my friends! We don't know the hour. But we don't have to worry about that if we know the Savior of the hour!

What is my future like?

That's a question a lot of kids probably would like to ask, because many kids have worries about their future. Have you heard this saying? I don't know who wrote it, but I like it a lot. I hope you do too! "We don't know what the future holds, but we know who holds the future!"

Aren't you glad we know God holds your future? He has plans for you. He promises that when things happen to you, he'll use them for your good (Romans 8:28). When God's people worry about their future, God gives them this wonderful promise. It's a promise for you too.

If you're someone who worries about the future, you might want to write the words from Romans 8:28 on a piece of paper and hang them somewhere where you can see them every day. I think then you'll look forward to the future because of the presence of God, who holds your future!

PRAYER PONDER POINT

Do you pray for your grandparents very often?

(A) Yes, because they are aging and my papa broke his ankle. (Aisha)

(B) Yes, especially my grandma since my grandpa died. (Corey)

(C) Yes, because they are getting older. (Bethany)

(D) Yes, I pray for their salvation and their health. (Ross)

(E) I pray for my grandparents often because they are older and not in good health. I worry about them dying. (Shannon)

(F) Yes, because I want them to know Jesus. (Dylan)

Grandparents and older adults need our prayers—for health problems, loneliness, getting older, difficulty taking care of their homes, and even their faith (or a need for faith).

Write some special prayer thoughts for your grandparents below. And maybe you could call them and ask for any special prayer requests they have. Give it a try. I have a feeling they'll be thankful you called!

_____

_____

_____

BIBLE VERSE
FILL-IN-THE-_____!

I can do _____ through Him who gives me strength.

What's the correct answer?

      (A) anything (Geoff)

      (B) everything (Deanna)

      (C) all things (Lauren)

      (D) all (Shannon)

I guess you noticed that all the answers are pretty much the same! And they are all correct (Philippians 4:13). With Jesus Christ, we can do all things that are God-pleasing. God doesn't want us to do things he wouldn't be happy about, but if something is pleasing to him, he will give us the strength to accomplish it. That's great news! Now try on these answers for size.

      (A) Anything God-pleasing!

      (B) Everything God-pleasing!

      (C) All things God-pleasing!

      (D) All that's God-pleasing!

WHAT QUESTION WOULD YOU LIKE TO ASK JESUS?
(SIXTH OF FIFTEEN)

Even though the question says "one question," Donna couldn't narrow it down that far. She simply said, "I'd ask him a whole bunch of things!"

Do you know why asking lots of questions is great? Because you can learn from the answers. If no one had any questions, what would we learn?

Do you know the story about Job that's in the Bible? He was a wealthy man with a large family and lots of animals and land. Most importantly, he had lots of love for God in his heart. But everything was taken from him through no fault of his own.

God knew Job would still love him—no matter what. And he was right. But Job still had questions. More than twenty-five times in the book of Job, he asks a "Why?" question. Why, God? Why did this happen? Why did you allow this? God didn't mind him asking the "why" questions. We can ask them, too. He wants us to ask, so we can look for his answers. He doesn't want us to ask without trusting him.

You ask questions in school to learn. In the same way, ask God anything you would like so that you can earn more about his ways, his love, and his will.

Ask away! Even if you want to ask a lot of things! Then look for his answers!

Megan said she'd like to ask Jesus, "Will you please make me without sin?" That's a big question for eight little words! And since the Bible has big answers, let's take a look at some verses:

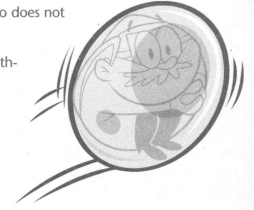

- There is no one who does not sin (1 Kings 8:46).

- If we claim to be without sin, we deceive ourselves and the truth is not in us (1 John 1:8).

- Who can say, . . . I am clean and without sin? (Proverbs 20:9).

All people sin when they disobey the will of God. But Jesus does give us a way out. Just take a look at these Bible verses:

- God made (Jesus) who had no sin to become sin for us, so that in him we might become the righteousness of God (2 Corinthians 5:21).

- (Jesus) takes away the sin of the world (John 1:29).

Jesus died to save us from sin. God forgives us our sins when we ask. So Christians are sure of one thing—when we go to heaven, Jesus does make us all without sin! How's that for a big answer?

WHAT QUESTION WOULD YOU LIKE TO ASK JESUS?
(EIGHTH OF FIFTEEN)

A very smart girl said she'd ask Jesus, "Do you love all the people that don't love you?"

What do you think the answer is to that question?

(A) Yes

(B) No

(C) Maybe

One of the most amazing things about our God, the one, true God, is that he loves all people—even those who don't love him. He proved that he loves us—every one of us—by sending Jesus to die on the cross to save us.

It's sad that some people will say "no" to his gift of forgiveness and eternal life. It's a gift! It's free to us, though it cost him everything. Some won't accept it, but he continues to love them and wants us to love them also and never give up on them.

Paul writes, "When you sin, the pay you get is death. But God gives you the gift of eternal life because of what Christ Jesus our Lord has done" (Romans 6:23 NIrV).

So keep praying! Keep loving! Continue to share the saving message of God's wonderful gift—even with those who don't love him . . . yet!

68

Why are you so serious?

What's up with people thinking Jesus never smiled or laughed? We have too many pictures showing Jesus looking very serious.

In my devo-writing lab is a set of pictures showing Jesus laughing and playing with children. And I have another one that shows him looking at me with eyes full of joy!

I know I shouldn't put words in Jesus' mouth, but here's what I think he might say to those who think he's very serious: "Yes, I'm serious about saving people. I'm serious about loving people. I'm serious about bringing people joy. I'm serious about giving hope. I'm serious about spending eternity with you in heaven. I'm serious about helping and caring for you. I'm serious about your sins and their consequences. But I'm also serious about forgiving your sins and taking away your guilt. I'm seriously interested in letting you know about the joy that's in my heart, and I want you to rejoice always!" I seriously think that's what he might say!

> Rejoice in the Lord always! I will say it again: Rejoice!
>
> PHILIPPIANS 4:4

Will I be able to go to my friend's house on Friday?

Some people need answers to deep, life-changing questions. Some have questions like Amanda's—simple, maybe not life-changing but weekend-changing. Amanda wants to know about her Friday plans. She wants to spend time with her friend. Do you think God cares about such a silly thing?

First of all, it's not silly! It's important to Amanda. And you know what that means? If it's important to Amanda (or you), it's important to God! He cares about you, all your questions, and everything you do!

Don't ever think anything is too small for God! Your questions aren't a bother to him. He cares about everything you do, think, and say! Is that cool, or what?

David, who wrote Psalm 8, stands in awe of this fact. He writes about how majestic God is, and then he asks God (in verse 4 NIrV), "What is a human being that you think about him?" We don't deserve his attention, but we have it!

LOL!
(LAUGHING OUT LOUD)

Stephen's favorite joke is:

> Q: If there are ten cats in a boat and one jumps out, how many are left?
>
> A: None. They were all copycats!

Excuse me a minute. D.J. is laughing so hard that he may need CPR. No, I think he's going to be okay. He's one unique critter—different from any lab assistant I've ever had!

We're all different, aren't we? We can thank God for that! We aren't all copycats. God created us with different looks, talents, and abilities.

We can celebrate the fact that we are different. We can also be happy God is always the same. Each one of us is important, and God wants to use our gifts to give him glory and help his kingdom grow.

First Corinthians 12:4–6 is a great section that talks about our differences. (If you want to be copycats, you can have someone else read it aloud after you!) Here it is: "There are different kinds of gifts, but the same Spirit. There are different kinds of service, but the same Lord. There are different kinds of working, but the same God works all of them in all men."

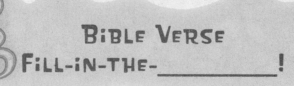

BIBLE VERSE
FILL-IN-THE-_____!

On the seventh day (of creation) God _____.

This must have been an easy fill-in-the-blank question because almost everyone I asked got it correct. The answer is "rested."

> By the seventh day God had finished the work he had been doing; so on the seventh day he rested from all his work. And God blessed the seventh day and made it holy, because on it he rested from all the work of creating that he had done.
>
> GENESIS 2:2–3

Did you notice it said God blessed the seventh day and made it holy? The word "holy" means "set apart." God set the day of rest apart from all the other days. It is supposed to be special. It is a time for us to find rest for our faith as we worship him. It's also a time to rest from work.

In the Old Testament, this day of rest was on Saturday. But after Jesus rose from the dead, the Christians began taking this day of rest on Sunday, to remember the resurrection of our Savior. This day of rest is set apart as special. Is Sunday special for you and your family, or is it like every other day of the week? How can you make it special?

Offer up a prayer thanking God for a day of rest and also for making this day especially holy.

Why does my family always fight?

In one way, the answer to that question is easy. It's because your family is made up of sinners, and sinners don't get along perfectly. People in churches fight because churches are made up of people who are sinners. It's the same for schools and places where your parents work. Sin is no fun. It ruins things. And the devil loves to tempt people to fight and argue.

> Pride only leads to arguing. But those who take advice are wise.
>
> PROVERBS 13:10 (niRv)

The only thing that will help is for Jesus to be brought into the middle of your family. If your family is always fighting, it's probably not praying together. There's probably a lot of selfish pride. Ask your family members to stop being proud and listen to each other.

Did you know that Christian counselors can give advice to families who fight all the time? Pastors may also be able to help. Start with prayer (which really means start with Jesus)! Jesus is the expert on sin problems because he offers the gift of forgiveness!

WHAT QUESTION WOULD YOU LIKE TO ASK JESUS?
(TWELFTH OF FIFTEEN)

As the computer in the Dr. Devo lab was putting together the information from the interviews we had with kids, it kept spitting one out. The computer said, "This does not compute! This does not compute!" D.J. and I took a look at the interview question and answer. The question was the one above: What one question would you like to ask Jesus? The computer showed us that some kids wanted to ask Jesus who they will marry when they get older.

I think I know why the computer said, "This does not compute!" It probably thinks you're too young to be worrying about who you're going to marry! Relax. God already knows who it will be—or even if there is someone. God's plan isn't the same for everyone. Some will be blessed with being single. That takes a special gift and person too.

But let's not throw that question out completely. There is something to be said here. What you can do is start praying that God prepares just the right person for you. Pray that person will be someone who has a great love for Jesus. Then pray that God will prepare you to be a godly marriage partner.

Pray. Trust. And relax! There's no need to worry now about who you're going to marry. But there is a need to pray about it during the years ahead!

Would you be my friend?

Kama, I hope you get to read this answer. Consider it as though coming from the very mouth of Jesus. Ready? Oh wait—one more thing. This answer is the same for everyone reading this. The answer is: Yes! Yes! Yes!

Got it? Jesus wants to be your friend now and for always. Have no doubt about it! John 15 talks about Jesus' friendship. Jesus told his disciples to "remain" in him (verse 7). This means to live in him, even when we can't see him, no matter where we are. He also told the disciples to keep his words inside themselves. And then he added, "You are my friends if you do what I command."

When we live in Jesus and let his words live in us, this friendship cannot be broken. He promises that when we obey him, we are his friends. Here are more of Jesus' own words, in John 15:15, "I no longer call you servants, because a servant does not know his master's business. Instead, I have called you friends."

Jesus shared these words with his disciples back then, but they are also for you and all his other disciples in this place and time. Friendship forever!

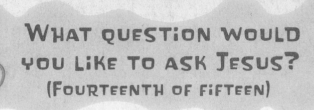

Can I have your autograph, please?

I have to ask, Derek, why you would want Jesus' autograph? Would it be because it would have such special meaning to you? Or would you want to try and sell it on the Internet and make gobs of money? I'm sure it's because it would be very meaningful to you! Or maybe you want him to sign that book he wrote? What's the name of it? Oh yeah, the Bible!

You may have to wait in line a long time for that autograph, my friend. But here is something you might find really cool! You and I are so meaningful to Jesus that he has engraved our names on the palms of his hands. Yep! He told his people, "See, I have engraved you on the palms of my hands." If you don't believe me, check it out in Isaiah 49:16! How cool is that!

The Lord has our autograph—in a way! And he won't try to sell it. We are his. He treasures each of us much more than we can imagine! He holds us in the palm of his hand, and he won't let go! Thank you, Jesus!

(By the way, Derek, can I have your autograph?)

WHAT QUESTION WOULD
YOU LIKE TO ASK JESUS?
(FiFTEENTH OF FiFTEEN)

How many hairs do I have?

Caitlyn may have wanted to ask that because Jesus mentions even the very hairs of our heads are numbered. He says that to show his people how special they are to him. He even loves our hair!

To research this answer, I went into the famous Dr. Devo library. I brushed off the cobwebs and started to comb the books for facts about hair. Then I found a book by another doctor (not a devotion doctor). It's a book I wasn't able to part with. I was glad I still had it; otherwise I would have had a hairy problem on my hands (and my head). I got right to the root of the answer.

Let's make a quiz out of this. On the average, how many strands of hair do you think a young adult has on his or her head?

(A) 350–500

(B) 1000–2500

(C) 100,000–150,000

(D) More than a million

Everyone have their guesses in? The answer is "C!" Hairs to the winners! Actually, knowing God cares about everything in and on our body as well as in our world means we are all winners in his sight!

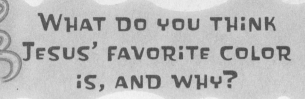

WHAT DO YOU THINK JESUS' FAVORITE COLOR IS, AND WHY?

Katie thinks it's blue because that's the color of the sky and when you're in heaven you're in the sky. Justin thought it might be red for courage and bravery. And Pamela thinks white could be his favorite because it's the color he sees when he washes away our sins.

Those are excellent ideas. Jesus probably doesn't have a favorite color. But colors can remind us about Jesus and our faith in him. They can be used to remind us of him whenever we see them in the world around us.

Think of some ways the different colors listed below can remind you of Jesus or your faith in him. Can you think of some Bible stories or verses that go with the colors? Have fun thinking with the rainbow in your mind!

Red:
_____

White:
_____

Green:
_____

Blue:
_____

Purple:
_____

The colors in a rainbow:
_____

PRAYER PONDER POINT

When I asked kids to write a prayer of thanks to God, here are some of the responses I received:

(A) Jenny wrote, "Thank you for everyone and everything! Thank you for being you!!!"

(B) Amanda prayed, "Oh Dear Jesus, I love you and thank you for everything!"

> Give thanks to the Lord, for he is good; his love endures forever.
>
> PSALM 118:1

(C) And Gus said, "Thank you for everything in the world—for the birds in the sky and especially for you, God. Amen."

Everyday is a day of thanksgiving for Christians! Make a list below of things and people you are thankful for today. Then share a prayer of thanksgiving to God.

_____ _____

_____ _____

_____ _____

_____ _____

_____ _____

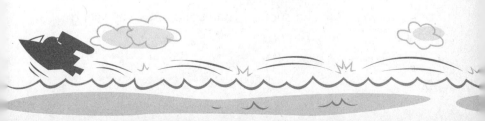

LOL!
(Laughing Out Loud)

Mom: Tommy, please put some water in your fish tank.

Tommy: Why, Mom? I put some in yesterday, and he hasn't drunk all of it yet!

Tanks for that fish tale, Tommy! That joke may hold water, but so does the story of Jesus and the Samaritan woman at the well found in John 4:5–26 is true. Jesus was talking to a woman at a well where she had come to get drinking water. Jesus wanted her to know about a different kind of water—the living water he came to bring.

We need water to live, right? Well, Jesus wanted her to know that if she would follow him, her faith would never get thirsty again. She'd live forever! She was looking for hope and help in the wrong places. Jesus, the Living Water, had more hope and good news than she would ever want or need! It would overflow in her life!

Here's what Jesus said to her in verse 14 of that chapter: "Everyone who drinks this water will be thirsty again, but whoever drinks the water I give him will never thirst. Indeed, the water I give him will become in him a spring of water welling up to eternal life."

Spring to your feet and shout, "Thank you Jesus, my Living Water!"

Bible Verse
Fill-in-the-_____!

Before a _____ is on my tongue, you know it completely, O Lord.

Some of the answers left me speechless! Here's how some of you filled in that blank:

(A) Before a bump is on my tongue, you know it completely, O Lord. (Jessica #1)

(B) Before a piece of candy is on my tongue, you know it completely, O Lord. (Jessica #2)

(C) Before a song is on my tongue, you know it completely, O Lord. (Curtis)

(D) Before a word is on my tongue, you know it completely, O Lord. (Rosalie and others)

Which answer do you think is correct? According to Psalm 139:4, "word" is the missing word! Before we decide what we're going to say, God already knows it! That's an awesome thought! But the other kids were right too. Before you might get a bump on your tongue, he knows and cares about it! Before you put a piece of candy on your tongue, the sweet news is that Jesus knows what you're going to do. Jesus created all 10,000 of your taste buds (by the way, when you get old, you may only have about half that many). Before you sing, Jesus hears your song (hopefully it's one that is pleasing to him)!

Before a word is on my tongue, you know it completely, O Lord. That is a great word from God's word!

HOW MANY SINS DO YOU THINK YOU COMMITTED YESTERDAY?

That was the question I asked. Here are some of the answers I received:

(A) 5   (G) 600

(B) 10   (H) 10,000

(C) 20   (I) 1,000,000

(D) 33   (J) 1,000,000,000,000,000,000,000,000
                          (he said it was a bad day)

(E) 50   (K) D.J.'s favorite answer: TOO MANY!

(F) 100

Any sin is one too many. And we sin more than once a day! Too many! Too often we may think, "I've been good today, so I probably haven't sinned that much. I'm sure I did better than that kid." If you ever think like that, tell the devil to get out of your head! That isn't the truth. If you think it is, read this verse.

Suppose you keep the whole law but trip over just one part of it. Then you are guilty of breaking all of it.
JAMES 2:10 (NIRV)

That means if you only committed one sin, you would be guilty of breaking every law. Yikes! A million is sounding more like the right answer!

Give thanks the incredible love and power of God to forgive all our sins. (By the way, you'll want to read the devotion on the next page tomorrow. It's a good follow-up to this one!)

HOW MANY SINS DO YOU THINK JESUS FORGAVE YOU YESTERDAY?

That was the question I asked. Here are some of the answers I received:

(A) 5

(B) 10

(C) 20

(D) 33

(E) 50

(F) 100

(G) 600

(H) 10,000

(I) 1,000,000

(J) 1,000,000,000,000,000,000,000 (he said it was a bad day)

(K) D.J.'s favorite answer: TOO MANY!

If you haven't read the page before this one, do that now. The kids gave the same answers to both questions. They obviously know all about their forgiving God!

Here's what God's word has to say: "God is faithful and fair. If we admit that we have sinned, he will forgive us our sins. He will forgive every wrong thing we have done. He will make us pure." (1 John 1:9 NIrV).

Jesus didn't die for *some* of your sins. He didn't rise from the dead so you can be certain *most* of your sins will be forgiven. Jesus Christ died and rose from the dead so you can be sure that he gives total forgiveness to everyone who is sorry for his or her sins!

LOL!
(Laughing Out Loud)

Q: What fish doesn't make sense?

A: The piece of cod which transcends all understanding!

Funny stuff! Let me explain that joke for those of you who may not understand it. Philippians 4:7 says, "The peace of God which transcends all understanding . . . will guard your hearts and your minds in Christ Jesus." The joke is a play on words using that verse. Cod is a fish. Instead of saying, "The peace of God," the joke teller said, "The piece of cod."

Another Bible translation explains Philippians 4:7 this way: "God's peace can never be completely understood" (NIrV). Is that easier to understand? People say a joke isn't funny if you have to explain it because it doesn't mean anything to the person hearing it. That's probably true. But, hopefully, if someone has to explain a Bible verse, it can still mean a lot to you.

At times we can't understand why we feel peaceful. Maybe it's in the middle of a storm, or right before a test, or even when someone we know dies. That peace comes from God, and we can't explain it. It's a wonderful gift—it's the peace of God which transcends all our understanding!

DOES THE OLD TESTAMENT HAVE ANYTHING IN IT ABOUT JESUS?

Most kids answered that question with a "Yes!" That's the correct answer! Some didn't think so because Jesus wasn't born during Old Testament times. Since everything in the Old Testament is pointing toward Jesus, though, the entire Bible centers around him! All through the Old Testament, God made a promise that he would one day send a Savior, a Messiah. That would be Jesus.

Some verses of the Old Testament gave away "secrets" to the birth or life of this Savior. Here are a few:

- Isaiah 7:14: "Therefore the Lord himself will give you a sign: The virgin will be with child and will give birth to a son, and will call him Immanuel."

- Isaiah 53:5 (NIrV): "The servant was pierced because we had sinned. He was crushed because we had done what was evil. He was punished to make us whole again. His wounds have healed us."

- Micah 5:2: "But you Bethlehem . . . though you are small among the clans of Judah, out of you will come for me one who will be ruler over Israel."

- Zechariah 9:9: "Rejoice greatly, O Daughter of Zion! Shout, Daughter of Jerusalem! See, your king comes to you, righteous and having salvation, gentle and riding on a donkey."

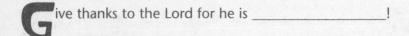

BIBLE VERSE
FILL-IN-THE-_____!

Give thanks to the Lord for he is _____!

And the answers given were:

    (A) ours! (Jess)

    (B) great! (Rosey)

    (C) fun! (Adam)

    (D) risen! (Thomas)

    (E) good! (Mandi and others)

All those answers rock! The words, "Give thanks to the Lord for he is good," appear in at least four different Psalms—106, 107, 118, and 136. The Psalm writers really wanted people to know the Lord God is good.

When I was your age, I always wondered why the Psalm writers didn't use a bigger word to describe the Lord. He is awesome! Amazing! Incredible! Super-duper! "Good" doesn't sound as exciting. God is amazing and awesome. But he is also good. And that is good for us! He is good to us and for us. And it is good to thank him for his goodness.

Tell everyone the good news: The Lord is ours! He's great! He's forgiving! He's risen! Give thanks for all those things! Give thanks . . . for he is good!

A Question
for David!

How did a little guy like
you kill a big bad man?

This devotion is dedicated to all the little people out there (and the little critters like D.J.)!

Ladies and gentlemen, boys and girls of all heights and sizes . . . In this corner, we have the mighty Goliath. He stands more than nine feet tall. Yes, that's right—nine feet tall! And I'd tell you how much he weighed, but he broke the scale! And in the other corner, is this kid named David. We won't even mention his height and weight!

But wait a minute, there's someone else in David's corner. It's the Lord God himself! Little guy David stands up straight and says to the big guy across the way, "I come against you in the name of the Lord Almighty . . . all those gathered here will know that it is not by sword or spear that the Lord saves; for the battle is the Lord's and he will give all of you into our hands" (1 Samuel 17:45, 47).

Does that answer your question, Donna? The battle was the Lord's! No wonder he won! David had some stones in his sling-shot but, more importantly, he had the Lord in his heart . . . and his corner!

ANOTHER QUESTION FOR DAVID!

Why did you play the harp?

David might answer that by telling you he loved the gift of music. Since the stringed harp has a peaceful sound, he'd probably say he played it to give God glory through music. He might also tell you he used it to calm himself and the sheep he watched during long, dark nights. David wrote songs, many of which are found in the book of Psalms. Not only was David's music a blessing to God, but God used his musical gifts to be a blessing to others.

When Saul was king (not the same Saul who later became Paul), he turned away from God, and an evil spirit tormented him. Saul's advisors suggested they find someone who could play some soothing music for the king. They called for David. The advisors told the king that David was "a brave man and a warrior. He speaks well and is a fine-looking man. And the Lord is with him" (1 Samuel 16:18). So David served Saul. Whenever the evil spirit bothered Saul, David played his harp, and the king felt better!

Do you have musical gifts? You never know how God is going to use your gift of music to praise Him or to be a blessing to others! Worship the Lord with the gift of music!

(D.J. just asked me if David played in the Jerusalem Marching Band! What a goof ball! Everyone knows you can't play a harp while you're marching!)

Yet Another Question for David!

Was it cool to be a king?

I wonder if David might answer Rachel with a letter something like this:

Dear Rachel,

Thanks for your question. In one way, it was very cool to be chosen by God to be king. I was just a shepherd boy, but God had such amazing plans for my life. I owe everything to him.

It's cool to follow God's plans for your life. I just loved him and let him lead—but there were some things that weren't very much fun. Leaders have lots of responsibilities. People didn't always agree with the way I did things. I faced jealousy, wars, staff problems, family problems, and so much more.

And sometimes I didn't handle things very well. Those were the times that I realized I was trying to do things on my own instead of letting God be the real king. That will always be a problem, I guess. People want to be king of their lives instead of letting God be king.

Your friend,

David
King of Israel

Thanks again for the question, Rachel! Remember to let God be King of your life!

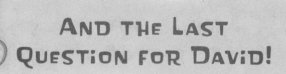

AND THE LAST QUESTION FOR DAVID!

Were you scared?

So many times in David's life, he could have been scared. Think of just a few of the situations he was in:

- As a shepherd, he had to keep wild animals away from the sheep.

- David fought against the giant, Goliath.

- King Saul tried to kill him.

- David led armies into battle.

- Nations of enemies surrounded him.

Those are just a few times David could have been scared! But he knew to run to the Lord to find peace and help. Check out these great words of faith from David:

- "I will not fear the tens of thousands drawn up against me on every side. Arise, O Lord! Deliver me, O my God!" (Psalm 3:6)

- "Even though I walk through the valley of the shadow of death, I will fear no evil, for you are with me." (Psalm 23:4)

- "The Lord is my light and my salvation—whom shall I fear? The Lord is the stronghold of my life—of whom shall I be afraid?" (Psalm 27:1)

Logan, thanks for the question! We can all thank God for men like David who teach us not to be afraid.

PRAYER PONDER POINT

Write a prayer asking God to help you with something you have to do soon.

When Kendra was given this assignment, here's the prayer she wrote:

Dear God, will you please help me trick or treat without hurting myself or getting in trouble or maybe getting scared by a stranger. If you would please do this, I would be very pleased. Amen.

I'm sure Kendra was very pleased with God's protection on a night when she was scared! In our last devotion, we read some great verses from David about trusting God, who can take away our fears.

Write down things that scare you. Then read the verses on page 92 again. Pray that you will trust God in all things. If you would please do this, God would be very pleased, I'm sure!

_____

_____

_____

_____

_____

_____

_____

A BIT ABOUT JOSEPH

Q: Hey Eddie, what do you think Jesus did when he was nine years old?

A: I think he worked with his stepdad.

That's a good thought, Eddie! Did all of you in devotion-reading land realize that Joseph was Jesus' stepfather? He was! Jesus was Mary's son, but born through the power of the Holy Spirit.

Maybe you've never thought about that before. It may not be a big deal for you, but for some kids it is. Lots of kids have step-dads or stepmoms. They may think Jesus wouldn't know what it's like to be a part of a stepfamily—but he does!

Some stepfamilies get along great. Others have a tough time. Do you have some friends who have stepparents? That can be a challenge for kids. Take time to pray for your friends today.

Jesus grew up doing the work of his stepdad, Joseph. Do you know what kind of work Joseph did? (I'm waiting for you to answer!) He was a carpenter. And that's what Jesus did too.

No matter how much woodwork Jesus did with his stepfather, his greatest work was the work he did on the wood of the cross, forgiving us and giving us life!

LOL!
(Laughing Out Loud)

Here's a riddle for you:

> Q: What can't ask questions but always wants an answer?
>
> A: A doorbell.

Okay, now choose a question below that you think Jesus always wants us to answer.

> (A) Why did the chicken cross the road?
>
> (B) Would you like some fries with that?
>
> (C) Will you follow me, live for me, and trust in me your whole life, knowing I am the only way to heaven?

Jesus doesn't have to ring the doorbell for us to answer that question! With Jesus as Lord of our lives, we have a best friend right inside our hearts. He's there to protect us and give us strength. He wants to help us in all we do. And he's always there to listen—no matter what kinds of questions we ask!

God is our refuge and strength, an ever-present help in trouble. Therefore we will not fear, though the earth give way and the mountains fall into the heart of the sea, though its waters roar and foam and the mountains quake with their surging.

Psalm 46:1–3

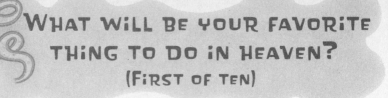

WHAT WILL BE YOUR FAVORITE THING TO DO IN HEAVEN?
(FIRST OF TEN)

This reporter got some interesting answers, including one from a girl who said her favorite thing would be playing with her dead snake! Yikes!

A nine-year-old wrote me and said her favorite thing to do in heaven would be "to see Jesus and be able to walk." I don't know her situation, but it sounds like she isn't able to walk now. She knows in heaven she will walk for sure! Revelation 21:5 says that in heaven Jesus will make everything new!

- Those who couldn't walk on earth will run, walk, skip, and jump in heaven!

- Those who can't speak will talk, sing, shout, and even yodel if they want!

- Those who can't see will joyfully see Jesus and all of heaven!

- Those who can't play the tuba will play it perfectly! (D.J. made me add that one!)

Is that new news to you? Even if it's not new, it's good news for sure!

WHAT WILL BE YOUR FAVORITE THING TO DO IN HEAVEN?
(SECOND OF TEN)

Kristen's favorite thing to do in heaven will be playing with Jesus! You read that right. It doesn't say "pray with Jesus." Kristen wants to "play" with Jesus. How cool will that be? Jesus loves kids. He loves to have fun. He loves to spend time with kids and adults. He loves you!

Remember what Mark 9:36–37 says? "Jesus took a little child and had him stand among them. Taking him in his arms, he said to them, 'Whoever welcomes one of these little children in my name welcomes me.'"

Put on your imagination hat and picture yourself in heaven running and jumping into Jesus' arms! Let him swing you around. Then . . .

- Give him a hug.
- Hear him tell you how much he loves you.
- Tell him how much you love him.
- Run through the streets with him.
- Do somersaults.
- Jump up and down with him.

What do you want to do? He's your Savior! You're home and Jesus wants to play with you!

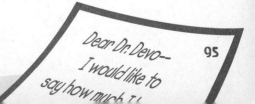

Dear Dr. Devo—
I would like to
say how much I

WHAT WILL BE YOUR FAVORITE THING TO DO IN HEAVEN?
(THIRD OF TEN)

Katie says she's looking forward to spending time hanging out with the angels! Not only do we get to spend eternity with Jesus but we also get to hang out with believers of every age and the angels too.

How cool will it be praising God perfectly with the angels who have been doing it since the beginning of time?

It will be amazing to sing with the angel choir (maybe you'll get to sing a solo)!

You can spend some time talking with Gabriel about when God pulled open the door to heaven and sent him to tell Mary she would be the mother of God's Son! Dude! That will be wild!

You can even get the perfect recipe for angel food cake!

Heaven will be perfect! Just one of the wonderful things to do there will be spending time hanging out with the angels. When they welcome us into heaven, I wonder if they'll say to us what Gabriel said to Mary, "Greetings . . . the Lord is with you."

WHAT WILL BE YOUR FAVORITE THING TO DO IN HEAVEN?
(FOURTH OF TEN)

Casey is looking forward to spending time with God. Awesome answer, Casey! That's what it's all about! And Casey, you'll have an eternity to spend time with him. No more busy schedules to worry about! You'll always have time for God. And he'll always have time for you!

You'll never stop wanting to spend time with him, and you'll never get bored while you're with him.

> Surely goodness and love will follow me all the days of my life, and I will dwell in the house of the Lord forever.
>
> PSALM 23:6

1. You'll spend time praising him. In fact, you'll worship him in everything you do!

2. You'll have quiet time with him, and time to just enjoy his presence!

3. You'll have time to sing, laugh, and shout with joy!

4. You'll have time for everything good in his presence . . . time without end!

WHAT WILL BE YOUR FAVORITE THING TO DO IN HEAVEN?
(FIFTH OF TEN)

Sarah thinks her favorite thing to do in heaven will be to look around! Ah, so much to see! So many people to see! Unfortunately, not everyone who ever lived on earth will be there because some will have rejected Jesus and will spend eternity away from God.

Most important, we'll get to look around and see Jesus! Take a look at what John got to see in his revelation about heaven. He writes this in Revelation 1:17–18: "When I saw him, I fell at his feet as though dead. Then he placed his right hand on me and said: 'Do not be afraid. I am the First and Last. I am the Living One; I was dead, and behold I am alive for ever and ever!'"

Imagine yourself standing in the middle of heaven. Pretend you're looking all around you. What and who do you see?

WHAT WiLL BE YOUR FAVORiTE THiNG TO DO iN HEAVEN?
(SixTH OF TEN)

Andrew let me know that his favorite thing about heaven will be living forever. D.J. and I think that's a pretty interesting answer. When I was about your age, Andrew, that was the hardest part for me to understand and look forward to about heaven. I think it was hard because my mind couldn't understand a life without an end.

We know that on this earth people die because sin is in the world. Since there won't be sin in heaven, there won't be any death either. That used to bother me when I was a kid because my mind couldn't understand it. But I finally realized there is so much I can't understand about God's perfect ways and his perfect heaven.

Heaven will be a zillion times better than your mind can imagine. He has prepared the very best for you and me—even though we don't deserve any of it! When you look at it that way, you can join Andrew in looking forward to living forever! You'll never have to say good-bye to anyone again. No more diseases. No more death. Only life because of Jesus, who is the resurrection and the life (John 11:25)!

Branden said, "Serving God! How cool! You have a servant's heart! You know we are called to serve God forever!

- We will serve him with our voices.

- We will serve him with our hands.

- We will serve him with our minds.

- We will serve him with our feet.

- We will serve him with our love.

- We will serve him with our worship.

- We will serve him constantly.

- We will serve him forever.

Like Psalm 17:11 says, "All kings will bow down to him and all nations will serve him."

Won't it be cool in the kingdom of heaven to hear Jesus say to you, "Hey kid, my kid, whom I love . . . nice serve!"

[Jesus has] made them to be a kingdom and priests to serve our God, and they will reign on the earth.

REVELATION 5:10

Deborah has a whole list of things she's looking forward to doing in heaven. She said that among her favorites will be:

- Meeting Bible characters.

- Seeing relatives.

- Praying and praising.

- Meeting God!

It's awesome to realize we will get to worship God with all believers—even those we've read about in the Bible! We'll also get to meet relatives we've never known. Obviously, the most important thing is we'll get to be with God!

Just for fun, think about these questions:

1. Who are five people from the Bible—now in heaven—who you look forward to meeting?

2. Who are five believers from any time in history that you look forward to seeing?

3. Who are some of the relatives you will enjoy seeing at this family reunion in heaven?

Be encouraged to read Hebrews 11. It includes a great history of people from the Bible who, by faith, followed God and will spend eternity in heaven with us!

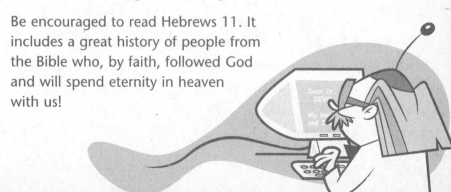

WHAT WILL BE YOUR FAVORITE THING TO DO IN HEAVEN?
(NINTH OF TEN)

Amanda didn't just say she's looking forward to playing in heaven, she said, "playing tag in the clouds!" That's an interesting thought! But I wouldn't want to play tag with David. He might tag me with his slingshot! Adam and Eve practiced hiding in the Garden of Eden, so they might be hard to find! Jonah is good at running away from people. Solomon is too smart to get caught. I think I might want to play tag with Paul in heaven. He got caught a lot (for telling the good news of Jesus) and put in jail!

Just for fun, think of these games you could play in heaven! (If you don't understand them, just ask your parents or a teacher!)

- SIMON (Peter) SAYS ("You are the Christ, the Son of the Living God." See Matthew 16:16)

- PIN THE WHALE ON THE JONAH

- MUSICAL HEIRS (We're heirs of God's heavenly gifts. See Romans 8:17)

- HIDE AND GO MEEK (The meek are blessed. See Matthew 5:5)

- GRACEBALL (Ephesians 2:8–9 is always a hit in this game!)

Isn't it great to have fun and get silly sometimes? We can do that and still be serious about the saving news of our Savior, whom we love! That's no game!

Krys has the right idea! Everything!

We can look forward to everything in heaven. It will be perfect! Everything will be perfect. We can look forward to it all! Everything will be our favorite thing to do!

If you believe in Jesus Christ as your Savior from sin and death, then there is nothing for you to fear about heaven. Jesus will stand in your place and say to his Father, "I died for this child. Judge this one on my perfect life." And God the Father will answer, "Because of Jesus, you are perfect! Enter my perfect heaven!"

Let's close this devotion with prayer together:

Thank you, Jesus, for making heaven possible for me. I'm looking forward to everything—especially being with you forever. Until that day, teach me to follow you. Strengthen my faith. Keep me close to you until I see you face to face!

LOL!
(LAUGHING OUT LOUD)

I think you might like this joke that Braeden sent to the Dr. Devo lab. Here goes:

Knock-knock.

Who's there?

Amos.

Amos who?

Amos Squito (A mosquito) who wants to bite you.

Amos is a book in the Bible about a man named Amos. I asked a team of kids, "What do you think Amos did for a job?"

- A moss collector. (Ha-ha, get it? A-moss!) But seriously, he was a prophet. (Nathan)

- A builder of buildings. (Matthew from Canada)

- A person who fought battles in God's name. (Andria)

- A farmer. (Emily from Illinois)

- Maybe he's that Famous Amos cookie guy! (Kirsten)

- Amos took care of sycamore-fig trees and was a shepherd. (D.J.)

Two of the above are correct. To find out which two, read Amos 7:14–15. When you do, remember that God can use you in any job to serve him and tell others about him!

WHAT WILL BE YOUR LEAST FAVORITE THING TO DO IN HEAVEN?

Dr. Devo's interview question got these responses:

- Falling through the clouds! (Henry)

- Not being lazy anymore. (Mark)

- Math. (Mallorie)

- Watching things. (Amanda)

- Nothing, because everything is great in heaven. (Pamela)

Pamela has the perfect answer because heaven will be perfect! There won't be anything bad or less than the best in heaven. That's hard to imagine, isn't it? But it's true. Henry won't get hurt in heaven! Mark won't miss being lazy in the least bit. Mallorie won't worry about math or anything else. And Amanda's eyes will be filled with perfectly perfect things to watch—forever!

Doesn't it rock that God loves us with an everlasting love? (Jeremiah 31:3)

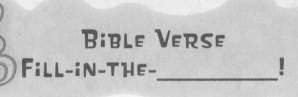

Bible Verse
Fill-in-the-_____!

The gift of God is _____ _____ Christ Jesus our Lord.

- love and peace (Dana)

- smartness and goodness (Nathaniel)

- so cool (Samiejo)

- eternal life (Susan and others)

All of those suggestions would fit, wouldn't they? Even the idea that the gift of God is *so cool* through Jesus Christ! All of God's gifts are so cool, including his gifts of love, peace, smartness, and goodness. But probably the coolest of cool gifts is God's gift of *eternal life* in Jesus Christ (Romans 6:23). Eternal life is a gift!

We don't deserve it. We deserve eternal death, like the first part of Romans 6:23 says. But it is so cool, amazing, incredible, and fantastic that God would give us what we don't deserve—to spend every moment with Jesus. And it's all because he loved us so much that he died and rose for us! That is so, so cool!

Thank God for all your gifts in life, especially the gift of eternal life, through Jesus Christ!

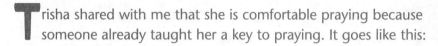

ARE YOU COMFORTABLE PRAYING?

Trisha shared with me that she is comfortable praying because someone already taught her a key to praying. It goes like this:

- *Pray* about things happening in your life.

- *Praise* the Lord for his work.

- *Give thanks* to the Lord for what he has done.

That's a great help, Trisha! Thanks for sharing that with the Dr. Devo readers! Pray. Praise. Give thanks.

Another key that might help you become more comfortable uses each letter of the word "PRAY."

- *P* raise (We have so much to praise God for—don't forget this important part of talking to God in prayer.)

- *R* epent (God wants us to repent—to tell him how sorry we are for our sins—and then to know we have his forgiveness through Jesus.)

> The prayer of a godly person is powerful. It makes things happen.
>
> JAMES 5:16b (NIRV)

- *A* sk (We can ask God anything. He wants what is best for us, and we can trust him to give us only what is helpful for our lives and faith.)

- *Y* ield (To yield means to give way to what God wants for our lives. We yield our will to him.)

WHAT DO YOU WORRY ABOUT?

Four kids (and D.J.) told me these things they worry about. How do they rate on your worry scale?

- Tornadoes. (Barrett)

- Getting in trouble. (Jeffrey)

- Bad guys. (Kristine)

- Spelling tests. (Courtney)

- Wild Boars. (D.J.)

Fill in this blank: "I worry about _____."

Everyone worries about something or other. Is worrying right or wrong? Which of the following do you think Jesus said?

    (A) "I tell you, do not worry about worrying. Everyone does it."

    (B) "I tell you, do not worry about your life."

    (C) "I tell you, even I worry about some things."

Look up Matthew 6:25 for the answer. Then look up to Jesus and pray,

> Forgive me when I worry about things.
> I want to trust in you in all things. I'm glad I don't have to worry about whether you love me! I know you do! I love you, Jesus. Amen.

WHAT'S YOUR FAVORITE FOOD?
(FIRST OF TWO)

Wow, my Dr. Devo mailbox was *flooded* with answers for this question! Dylan's favorite is brownies! Tyler has expensive tastes. His favorite is crab legs with melted butter! Some other answers: pizza, black olives, spinach, potatoes, chicken salad, watermelon, pears, hot dogs, chicken, and fruit. One person even said vegetables and daily bread!

God wants us to remember more than grace when hungry for our "daily bread." He wants us to remember that we do "not live by bread alone but on every word that comes from the mouth of the Lord" (Deuteronomy 8:3). This means we are fed through the word of God. Our favorite foods do fill our bellies, but it's the Bible that fills our hearts. Mmmm-good. In this way, we'll never go hungry!

WHAT'S YOUR FAVORITE FOOD?
(SECOND OF TWO)

Think of all the blessings, people, and maybe even companies that make it possible for you to eat your favorite and not-so-favorite foods. Try to work backward (all the way back to God, the Creator) to figure out how your favorite food gets to your mouth. Thank God for the people he uses to get food to you. For instance, if your favorite food is watermelon, thank God for your parents who bought the melon, the workers in the grocery store, the truck drivers who brought it to the store, the farm workers who picked it, the farmer who planted the seeds, the company that sold the farmer the seeds, and God who made the soil fertile and the seed grow, using his gifts of sun and rain. Think about it! What a blessing to have the foods we do to strengthen our bodies.

Then God said, "I give you every seed-bearing plant on the face of the whole earth and every tree that has fruit with seed in it. They will be yours for food."

GENESIS 1:29

Thank you, God, for making sure we have food to eat!

WHAT ARE YOU THINKING ABOUT DOING FOR WORK WHEN YOU GROW UP?

I found two kids who will be very busy when they grow up, if they do everything they want to! Jacob wants to be a teacher, a firefighter, and a meteorologist. And Jessica wants to be a singer, actress, model, and a doctor for children and women!

If Jacob and Jessica do all that in their adult lives, they're going to be very busy and very educated!

Lots of people change jobs during their lives. For instance I, Dr. Devo, used to be a fireman—until I got *fired*! Then I had a job at a one-hour photo place, but my boss said I acted too positive to work with *negatives*! Next I worked in a muffler factory, but that was *exhausting*! Then I became a history teacher, but realized there was *no future* in it. I also had a job in a shoe store for a while, but I just didn't *fit in*. After that I fixed bathtubs and sinks, but that work was *draining*. Finally, God called me to write devotions for you! I said "All *write*, God, I'd love to do that!"

No matter what kind of work you do—around the house now or as job in the future—remember what God's Word says in Colossians 3:23, "Whatever you do, work at it with all your heart, as working for the Lord, not for men."

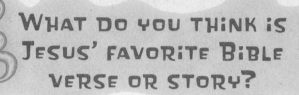

WHAT DO YOU THINK IS JESUS' FAVORITE BIBLE VERSE OR STORY?

Christina thinks it's the story of Adam and Eve. Katy thinks it's the story of Jesus' birth because it's fun learning about when we were little. And Eddie, a creative speller, thinks it might be the story of "creyashon."

D.J. and I aren't sure what Jesus' favorite Bible story might be, but eight-year-old David has a good thought. He thinks it might be found in John 3:16: For God so loved the world that he gave his one and only Son, that whoever believes in him shall not perish but have eternal life. Good answer, David! This may be the most powerful verse in the Bible.

When Jesus said those words, he was teaching a man named Nicodemus how to be saved. Sometimes when we share the good news, people can ask tough questions. Nicodemus sure did! Notice the ways Jesus shows us how to answer these questions in John 3.

Think about your own favorite verse in the and how you can use it to spread the good news of eternal life!

ANOTHER QUESTION FOR MARY, JESUS' MOM

Were you sad when you had to have your baby in a stable?

The Bible doesn't give the answer to Emilie's interesting question. How would you answer it? You would probably want better for the birth of a baby. But if you knew your own child would be the world's Savior, you would *really* want the best, wouldn't you!

Even though Mary and Joseph wanted the best for Jesus, I think they knew and trusted that God was in charge. We can also remember how Mary responded when the angel told her she was pregnant with Jesus. Mary told the angel, "I am the Lord's servant. May it be to me as you have said" (Luke 1:38).

When she found out Jesus' first bed would be a manger, Mary may have prayed something like, "Father God, I don't understand why this is happening this way, but I trust you. I know you are in charge. You have a reason and will use it for good. I am your servant. May this all be as you have planned, not as I want."

What do you need to fully trust God about today?

WHAT LANGUAGE DO YOU THINK THE BIBLE WAS WRITTEN IN?

The answers with the most votes were:

(A) Hebrew

(B) Greek (One person even wrote "Geek," but I think they meant "Greek"!)

(C) Latin

(D) Jewish

One voted for Japanese Hebrew!

What would you vote for? (I'm waiting for you to vote!)

Two answers are correct: The Old Testament was originally written in Hebrew, and the New Testament was written in Greek—not Geek! But D.J., my trusty lab assistant, just interrupted me and asked, "Isn't the Bible written in God's language?" Hmmm. Good thought, D.J., my friend!

> The heavens declare the glory of God; . . . There is no speech or language where their voice is not heard.
>
> PSALM 19: 1-4, 3

In fact, 2 Timothy 3:16 says something about that. It tells us that all Scripture (the Bible) is inspired by God or, as some translations say, it's God-breathed. God led the writers to put in the truth. He used their talents and writing styles, inspiring them to write what they did. That does sound like God language, doesn't it? By the way, remember to pray for people who are translating God's Word into other languages so everyone can know of Jesus' good news!

LOL!
(Laughing Out Loud)

Knock-knock.

Who's there?

Knock-knock.

Who's there?

Knock-knock.

Who's there?

Little kid who can't reach the doorbell!

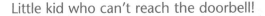

What are your arms too short to reach? In a great story in the Old Testament book of Numbers (11:21–23) Moses is kind of complaining to God. Moses doesn't think he can handle a situation, so he starts whining instead of trusting God. I can picture God shaking his head as he says to Moses, "Is the Lord's arm too short?"

That's what God said! What do you think he meant? In saying that, God reminded Moses nothing is impossible. God can reach down into any situation and solve any problem. He has the strength and power to handle what Moses couldn't deal with. You can be sure that his arm is long enough to help you handle your problems too.

Knock-knock.

Who's there?

Our God—with arms long enough to handle anything!

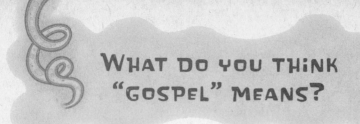

WHAT DO YOU THINK "GOSPEL" MEANS?

Have you heard the word "gospel" before? The word "gospel" means "good news."

When I asked Matthew about the meaning of this word, he said, "Some special books with special meaning." The Bible contains four special books called "The Gospels." They are the first four books of the New Testament—Matthew, Mark, Luke, and John. In a way, they have special meaning because these books tell us about the entire life of Jesus. The first verse of Mark says, "The beginning of the gospel (good news) about Jesus Christ, the Son of God." Jesus' life, words, and love are the good news!

Ashley wrote me that "gospel" is the opposite of "law." Good job, Ashley! That's another way to describe it. The law (God's commands) shows us our sin. The Gospel shows us our Savior—the saving good news of Jesus! God's law reminds us we are sinners. The good news or gospel is that Jesus saved us from our sin. He forgives us, loves us, and wants to give us heaven!

Mac described "gospel" as the Word of God. Sometimes, the entire Bible is called "gospel" because it tells of the good news of God and his love through Jesus! You might not find much "gospel" in today's news report, but the Bible is filled with it! Isn't that good news?

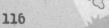

WHAT DO YOU THINK IS THE HARDEST JOB IN THE WORLD? (FIRST OF TWELVE)

It didn't take Sarah long to come up with her answer . . . "Being a mom!" Right on, Sarah! Mike, Bethany, Tessa, and Jordin agree, as they said "being a parent" is the hardest job in the world. Being a mom or dad isn't easy!

Can you imagine living by yourself without a parent or someone in your life acting as your parent? How would you eat? Who would buy your clothes? Who would help you make important decisions? Who would make you take care of yourself? Your teeth would probably be rotten, you'd probably stink, your brain might be almost empty, and you might not even know about Jesus! What a mess!

Can you imagine being responsible for someone else's life? That's what parents do! God has asked moms and dads to take care of his children for him. And the job doesn't involve pay, like other jobs! A parent's pay is a child's smile, hug, respect, and the words "I love you!" Parenting is a special calling that can be very difficult. But taking care of God's children is also a joy.

Please pray for your parents! Ask them each day how you can pray for them. Thank them for teaching you about Jesus. And remember what God says to his forgiven children, "Honor your father and your mother" (Exodus 20:12).

WHAT DO YOU THINK IS THE HARDEST JOB IN THE WORLD? (SECOND OF TWELVE)

I put Samantha's answer in, and the computer answer terminal gave it a grade of "I-H" for "*Interestingly Honest.*" Samantha thinks that telling others about God is tough. Why do we sometimes find it so hard to tell others about God? We should want everyone to know how Jesus saved them so they can live forever in heaven. Part of our purpose on earth is to tell others about the saving good news of Jesus until everyone in the whole world knows.

We won't hide [the stories of God] from our children. We will tell them to those who live after us. We will tell them about what the Lord has done that is worthy of praise. We will talk about his power and the wonderful things he has done.

PSALM 78:4 NIrV

If you find it hard to tell others about Jesus, think of it this way. What other things are great news? Maybe getting an autograph from your favorite sports player, getting a horse, winning a free trip to anywhere, or getting to zoom around the world using Dr. Devo's jet ship? Could you keep *that* good news to yourself? Of course not! The news about Jesus is absolutely the very best news ever! It's all about his love and forgiveness, and that makes it much easier to tell everyone, "I know the Savior personally, and he wants you to know him too!"

D.J. and I salute Rachel for her answer. She thinks the hardest job in the world is fighting in a war. She's right that serving in the military is a very difficult job. Men and women serve their country and us so we can have special freedoms. They are willing to give up their lives, if necessary, for their country.

Jesus tells us in John 15:13, "Greater love has no one than this, that he lay down his life for his friends." Jesus did that for us. His victory over sin, Satan, and death is greater than winning any battle on earth. We get to spend our lives thanking him.

We also want to thank all those who have served in the military or are serving now. Put together a special prayer list for those you know who are serving our country. Pray for their family members who love them.

Prayers for those in the military:

_____

_____

_____

_____

_____

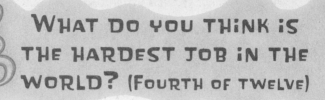

Both Gus and Allison think that being the president or leader of a nation is the toughest job around. That's a good answer. I know how hard it was to be president of my fourth grade Devotion Club (D.J. was the vice-president). That Devo club only had five members. I can't imagine being the leader of a whole nation! Yikes!

The leaders of every nation need our prayers! One thing we can pray for is that they will realize Jesus is the true leader of every nation. In the Old Testament, God's people wanted a king like the other nations. The Lord said he was their king. But they insisted they wanted someone else—their own human king.

The Lord knew it wasn't best for them, but since they insisted, he agreed to let them have one. This caused problems for centuries! We need to pray that all leaders will look to God to lead them. As you pray for world leaders, what else might you pray for?

Read 1 Samuel 8 to learn the story of the people who wanted their own king in Old Testament times.

WHAT DO YOU THINK IS THE HARDEST JOB IN THE WORLD? (FIFTH OF TWELVE)

When we saw Jenny's answer to this question, D.J. and I knew we wouldn't throw it in the garbage. Jenny thinks being a trash collector is the hardest job in the world. She's got a good point. Most people don't fully appreciate the work of trash collectors. They have to get up really early. They work outside in the heat of summer and the cold of winter. And they have to deal with our smelly, stinky garbage.

Think of all the things we throw in the garbage for them to deal with: the green, moldy stuff in the back of our refrigerators, slimy banana peels, rotten pumpkins, chewed gum, old bandages with blood, the tissues we blow our noses into—enough already! You get the idea! Can you imagine letting all that trash pile up in our house? Yuck!

We need to throw something else out—anything that we love more than the one true God. Sometimes we don't even know we have these 'gods' (spelled with a small letter 'g') in our lives. Joshua once told God's people, "Now then, throw away the gods that are among you. . . . Give yourselves completely to the Lord, the God of Israel" (Joshua 24:23). If you love something more than God, just throw it away!

The next time you see the people who collect your garbage, let them know you appreciate them and the work they do. And it's also a good idea to tell them that Jesus appreciates them too!

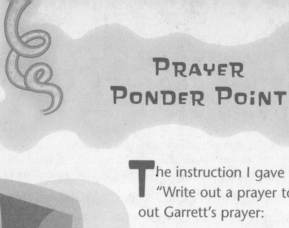

PRAYER
PONDER POINT

The instruction I gave was easy. I said, "Write out a prayer to Jesus." Check out Garrett's prayer:

> Dear Jesus,
> I love you.
> Amen.

His prayer is short, simple, pure, truthful, important, and deep. It's a great prayer. It says so much with just a few words. It tells the story of Jesus' love for Garrett and Garrett's love for his Savior. You see, Garrett (or any of us) couldn't love Jesus if Jesus hadn't first loved him (or us). That's why 1 John 4:19 tells us, "We love because he first loved us."

Garrett's prayer says it all. It tells about the important relationship he has with Jesus. It tells about his faith. It gives glory to God, who created love within him. It's a prayer that changes Garrett's life.

Will you pray that prayer also?

Josh was amazing when he said the hardest job in the world is building houses on Mars. He said it's the hardest because no one has done it yet! How can I argue with that? The last time D.J. and I were on Mars, we didn't see any houses. Of course, we were only on one side of the red planet.

Something that hasn't been done isn't necessarily the hardest job. If it were, we could use that excuse for anything we've never done before. I've never painted a picture of the ocean. I've never sung a solo in church. Remember what Paul wrote in Philippians 4:13, "I can do everything through [Christ] who gives me strength."

With God's strength, we can do all things that are pleasing to him—even if that includes building a house on Mars. What do you think about that, Josh?

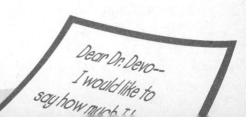

Dear Dr. Devo—
I would like to say how much I...

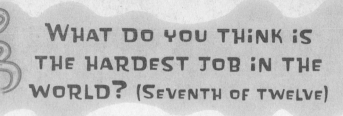

Being a firefighter! That's Angela's answer, and it's a good one. Fighting fires must be a very difficult job! I have a hard enough time blowing out the candles on my birthday cake! Please take time to pray that God will protect those who fight fires, as well as the police forces and emergency teams out on the roads! Write down some specific things for which you can pray.

_____

_____

_____

_____

Before you pray, remember that the devil wants to burn up your faith. He wants you to stop believing in Jesus. The apostle Paul tells us to put on the armor of God, including a shield of faith. Ephesians 6:16 says, "Take up the shield of faith, with which you can extinguish all the flaming arrows of the evil one."

A shield protects us—like the windshield in the car protects us from the wind. Our faith can become a shield, too—strong enough to protect us from the devil.

As you pray for firefighters, police officers, and emergency workers, pray that their faith will be strong in Christ Jesus.

Kenny did some deep thinking before he gave his answer to this question. He thinks the hardest job in the world is to die for someone.

I guess dying for someone isn't a job, but we all know someone who has done this—for us! His name is Jesus. Hebrews 12:2 says about Jesus, "Who for the joy set before him endured the cross ..." It says, who for the *joy*, not *job*, set before him. Jesus knew what came after the cross. That was pure joy for him. So dying on the cross wasn't a job. In one way, it was a joy.

It was a joy because it meant that all who believe in him as their Savior get to spend eternity with him—on earth and then in heaven. That made him happy. If dying for us could make that happen, then he would take on that job ... that calling ... that joy. What a Savior we have! What a joy to know him and his perfect love for us!

WHAT DO YOU THINK IS THE HARDEST JOB IN THE WORLD? (NINTH OF TWELVE)

Ethan said the hardest job in the world is to forgive people. It can be hard to forgive, especially when it looks like people are hurtful on purpose. But Jesus wants us to forgive others the same way he forgives us. It's usually our own feelings and actions that keep us forgiving. The apostle Paul lists some of these in Ephesians 4:31 (NIrV):

- hard feelings
- anger
- rage
- fighting
- lying
- hatred

What does Paul say about these feelings? Get rid of them! Stop it! And put it all away! Maybe you could imagine a giant pink eraser to help those feelings disappear—because forgiveness is on the other side of those feelings. Notice what Paul says next: "Be kind and tender to one another" (verse 32). When you erase your own bad feelings and actions, then kindness and tenderness are in your reach! And then Paul gives us the most powerful part of his message: "Forgive each other, just as God forgave you because of what Christ has done"

Pray to Jesus, asking him to help you find kindness and tenderness inside you. Let Jesus be like the giant pink eraser in your heart. Thank him for his gift of forgiveness. And ask him to help make it easier for you to forgive others, too.

Imagine some big bully walking up to you when you're all alone. He or she says something like this: "Hey, punk! You know I can't stand you. I can't stand the way you look, the way you smell, the way you walk. Is that a nose on your face or an extra big punching bag? Where'd you get those clothes—hand-me-downs from your great-grandmother?"

I hope no one ever talks to you that way and that you're never tempted to talk like that to anyone. It would be hard not to talk back in a mean way to someone like that. I guess that's why Jonathan told the Dr. Devo interview team he thought the hardest job in the world is to say nice things to enemies.

You can be sure of one thing. Someone who treats others like that has a lot of problems to deal with. Problems you can't imagine!

Jesus says to "love your enemies. Do good to those who hate you. Bless those who call down curses on you. And pray for those who treat you badly" (Luke 6:27-28 NIrV).

Go ahead! Show that bully the love of Jesus within you. His or her heart may be changed forever. It's not easy. But the results may be amazing, even if you don't see them right away.

Brandon should get the "MVA" award for his response to this question. ("MVA" stands for Most Valuable Answer!) To Brandon the hardest job in the world is being God! How can anyone top that? Can any of us even imagine what it would be like to be God? No, in our wildest dreams, we couldn't even come close!

Just for fun, imagine you are God. What would you do right now? We might think it's fun playing God but it's no joke. The problem is we play God every day, without even thinking about it. We do that when we want to be in charge, when we want everything our way. We trust ourselves more than we trust in God. We think we can do things on our own, without him. In other words, we make gods out of our bodies and minds. That breaks the first commandment, which says, "You shall have no other gods before me."

God's MVA (Most Valuable Answer) to our sin of playing God is how he offers forgiveness to all who repent. Congratulations on receiving God's MVA! Hold on to it tightly!

This is the last in this series about the hardest job in the world. Would you hand me a tissue, please? I think I may cry. (Sniffle, sniffle.) But wait! I'm looking at Paije's answer. Now I'm smiling! Forget the other answers—being in the military, a fire-fighter, a trash collector, a parent, forgiving people, or even being God! Paije is pretty sure that the hardest job in the entire world is (are you ready for this?) . . . cleaning the basement! Paije must have one huge, messy basement! I guess whatever job we have could seem like the hardest one ever.

But Brendan has another angle. He thinks that all jobs are hard! That's a pretty smart answer. Everything we do takes concentration, effort, and the desire to do our best. That's hard. But thankfully, we have God's help in whatever job we do. If God hadn't created our bodies and brains and given us abilities, we couldn't do anything! Jesus told his disciples, "apart from me you can do nothing" (John 15:5).

All jobs—large or small—are important. But we can praise God by doing every job we're given to the best of our ability.

LOL!
(Laughing Out Loud)

Q: Which bug runs away from everything?

A: A flee.

That was a tough one! What makes you flee (run away)? Can you think of a time when Jesus' disciples ran away? They must have been really scared. Something bad was happening. It was nighttime. Figured it out yet? It was when Jesus was arrested (for doing nothing wrong). Judas betrayed Jesus by bringing the chief priests, the teachers of the law, and the soldiers. Mark tells us that "everyone deserted him and fled" (14:50). They fled like a bunch of scared fleas running from a flea market!

After Jesus was crucified, rose from the dead, and ascended into heaven, the disciples' faith really started to grow. They received the gift of the Holy Spirit at Pentecost, and they didn't "flea" from things anymore. They stood up proudly for Jesus Christ. They weren't ashamed to talk about him or defend him. They went to prison for knowing him. Many of the disciples were even killed when they told others about him. How brave the Holy Spirit made them!

Say a prayer asking the Holy Spirit to strengthen your faith so you'll be strong like the disciples were—after they got over their flee problems!

BIBLE VERSE
FILL-iN-THE-_____!

Inside the fish, Jonah _____.

What do you think is the right answer? Julie said, "Jonah slept."
Kate told me that inside the fish "Jonah lived." Matt thinks "Jonah
thought!" Allie said, "Jonah repented." And many Dr. Devo readers said that "Jonah prayed." According to Jonah 2, that's exactly
what Jonah did.

Something else that you may not know is that Jonah gave thanks
to God. In part of his prayer he said, "But I, with a song of
thanksgiving, will sacrifice to you. What I have vowed I will make
good (verse 9). Even though he was sitting in the belly of a huge
fish that God had created, Jonah gave thanks because he knew
the Lord was in charge and could change his heart. We need to
remember that however bad things may seem, we need to trust
in God and ask him to use that bad situation to teach us to follow
him more closely.

By the way, after Jonah
prayed, you know what the
Lord did? He commanded
the big fish to vomit
Jonah onto the dry
land. Ewwww! Well,
he had to get
Jonah out of there
somehow! I think
I'm going to
forget about
swimming in the
ocean for a while!

WHAT WAS JESUS' FIRST MIRACLE MENTIONED IN THE BIBLE?

I zipped in the Dr. Devo jet ship across the country to get my friends' answers to this question. I dropped in on Carla, who said that Jesus' first miracle was making the earth. Then I stopped to see Josh, who told me that Christ's first miracle was being born of the Virgin Mary. And when I asked Emily, she said it was when Jesus turned water into wine.

Wow! I've got some smart friends! In a way, they're all correct. Although Jesus wasn't known as "Jesus" when the world began, he was one with God even back then, so he took part in creation. And when he became human as well as God, his birth to the Virgin Mary was an amazing miracle! But check out the miracle Jesus performed at a wedding in John 2. When he changed water into wine, this became "the first of his miraculous signs . . . He thus revealed his glory, and his disciples put their faith in him" (verse 11).

Jesus had some smart friends, too! When you think about it, everything about Jesus was a miracle—from his birth, through his life and ministry, and to his death and resurrection. It's a miracle that he lives today. And it's a miracle that he offers everlasting life to all who put their faith in him. He always has room for smart friends!

PRAYER PONDER POINT

What is a prayer warrior?

Paul told me that a prayer warrior is someone who prays for his or her enemies. Christopher said it's someone who is a great pray-er. Both young men are right. Prayer warriors spend a lot of time in prayer. They love to pray for others. They go to battle, as prayer warriors, against Satan's temptations, lifting others up to God. Part of their ministry of following Jesus is praying, praying, and more praying.

First Thessalonians 5:17 tells us to pray continually, without stopping, and always give thanks. Our whole lives are a prayer of thanks to God! Do you know someone who is a prayer warrior?

And what about this—prayer warriors need prayer too! Here's a short list of things you can pray as you lift them up to God, in the name of Jesus:

- Pray they will see God's answers to their prayers.

- Pray they will have great joy in praying for others.

- Pray they don't get discouraged in their prayer lives.

- Pray they will know God's will in who they pray for and what they pray for.

- Pray their faith will be strengthened every day.

Thank you, Jesus, for prayer warriors all over the world! Teach me to pray continually! Amen.

LOL!
(LAUGHING OUT LOUD)

Q: Why did the whale cross the road?

A: To get to the other tide!

Whale, what did you think of that joke? It cracks me up!

Have you ever seen whales swimming in the ocean? It's so cool. They are amazing creatures that God has made. And the ocean is even more amazing. If you've been to the ocean, you know about high tides and low tides. You have seen the waves just keep on waving, no matter what. The water is home to millions of creatures. It's such a miracle. I also have fun putting on my Dr. Devo swim suit and waterproof lab coat to play in the ocean.

The next time you see the ocean or any other body of water think about how important it is to life on earth. A psalm writer wrote about the water of the sea giving praise to God, with its waves, power, sound, and tides. He wrote, "Lord, the seas have lifted up their voice. They have lifted up their pounding waves. But Lord, you are more powerful than the roar of the ocean. You are stronger than the waves of the sea. Lord, you are powerful in heaven" (Psalm 93:3–4).

Let's join the ocean in giving God a whale of praise!

WHAT IS YOUR FAVORITE THING GOD MADE, AND WHY?

Andrie had a quick answer to this question. Her favorite thing God made is water! Andrie says she loves to play in water!

Water was important to Jesus too. Calvin Miller, a Dr. Devo friend, once thought of six things Jesus did with water:

1. He was baptized in it.

2. He changed it (water into wine).

3. He walked on it.

4. He ordered it around (when he told the sea to be still).

5. He claimed to be it (when he said he was life-giving water).

6. He drank it.

What have you done with water? We can pray with amazement and thanks to the one who can walk on water, change it, order it around, and even say he is living water! We can also be baptized, as Jesus commands. If you haven't been baptized, talk to your pastor about it.

You can read about the baptism of Jesus in Matthew 1:13–17. When Jesus was baptized a voice from heaven said, "This is my Son, and I love him. I am very pleased with him." Know that Jesus, the Living Water, also loves you. He is pleased with you, as well! Splash around with that good news for a while!

135

IF JESUS LIVED ON EARTH TODAY, WHAT WOULD HE WEAR?

How cool are these answers?

- Pants that fit and Nike shoes. Jesus, he said, would NOT wear saggy pants! (Matthew)

- Jeans and a cool shirt. (Christina)

- A robe. (Eric)

- Cargo pants and a white T-shirt, white tennis shoes, a baseball hat, and sunglasses. (Liz)

- A tuxedo. (Pamela)

- A shirt that has a picture of a cross, blue jeans, and a cross necklace. (Lisa)

- He'd be stylin'! (Chad)

D. J. and I don't know what Jesus would wear, but we know what he wants us to wear. Paul writes in Romans 13:14 that we should put on the Lord Jesus Christ as our clothing!

PSSSSST

So pull on his love. Slip into his happiness. Button up with the forgiveness of the Savior! Stay warm by wearing his kindness. Clothe yourself with everything Christlike. Wearing Christ out into the world is a perfect fit!

BIBLE VERSE
FILL-IN-THE-_____!

The Lord gave and the Lord has taken away; may the name of the Lord be _____.

Here are four choices to fill-in-the-blank. Which would you pick?

(A) With you (Steven)

(B) Holy (Christine)

(C) Glorified (Allie)

(D) Praised (Haley)

Although they could all be true, the answer is found in Job 1:21. It comes right after Job—who had ten children, thousands of animals, and a big house—got some very bad news. His children were killed. So were his animals. And his house was destroyed.

Right after all this he said, "The Lord gave and the Lord has taken away; may the name of the Lord be ____." What? If you agree with Haley, you're right. The answer is, "May the name of the Lord be praised!"

That has to be one of the most incredible things anyone ever said! Everything was taken from him, but he still praised the name of the Lord. What a great example of faith for us! Oh, he was sad. He probably cried. He missed his children, for sure. But he also praised God's name. He trusted in God. And in the end, because Job kept trusting him, God doubled all that he once had.

That's quite a story. Job had a great faith. But Job also had a great God—and he's your God too! May you always praise his name!

WHAT IS YOUR FAVORITE CHRISTIAN SONG?
(FIRST OF TEN)

Deb's favorite is the hymn "Beautiful Savior." It's a simple song that simply gives praise to the beauty of Jesus, our Savior. It's a song about giving praise to Jesus and also giving him our lives. Music is a wonderful gift. We have a wonderful gift in Jesus. And we have a great invitation to give him our lives, our love, and our thanks.

I don't know if you like to sing or not, but why don't you think about singing "Beautiful Savior" with your family or your classmates (if you're reading this in school). Don't be shy! God doesn't mind how your voice sounds; he loves to hear you sing his praise with whatever voice you have. Come on; do it for him! At least hum it and pray the words to him in your thoughts! Two verses of the hymn go like this:

Beautiful Savior, King of creation,
Son of God and Son of Man!
Truly I'd love thee, Truly I'd serve thee,
Light of my soul, my joy, my crown.

Beautiful Savior, Lord of the nations,
Son of God and Son of Man!
Glory and honor, praise, adoration
Now and forevermore be thine!

WHAT IS YOUR FAVORITE CHRISTIAN SONG?
(SECOND OF TEN)

One of Kirsten's favorite Christian songs is the Easter hymn "Christ is Risen, Alleluia." She likes it because it is quick and lively and has a pretty melody. It should be lively, like Kirsten said, because it's about a lively, living Jesus who once was dead but now lives! Can you imagine a slow, sad Easter song about Jesus' coming back to life after his crucifixion? That wouldn't make sense!

It's great to sing about Jesus' resurrection in every season of the year, not just in the Spring. Christ is risen! Alleluia! That news makes a difference every day of our lives! Because Jesus lives, all who put their faith in him will live—forever in heaven! That is so cool!

By the way, do you remember what "Alleluia" or "Hallelujah" means? It means "Praise the Lord!"

Christ is risen! Praise the Lord! Praise him with lively, pretty songs!

Hum, sing, whistle a tune! Jesus lives for you! Alleluia!

WHAT IS YOUR FAVORITE CHRISTIAN SONG?
(THIRD OF TEN)

Amanda mentioned one you might not think of as a song. She said she sings "The Lord's Prayer" a lot. Do you speak or sing the Lord's Prayer often? It's a model for all our prayers. It covers everything. When the disciples wanted Jesus to teach them to pray, he taught them "The Lord's Prayer" (Matthew 6:9–13 and Luke 11:2–4).

This would be a great time to sing (or speak) "The Lord's Prayer." Pause after each section to think about the meaning of the words. If you're reading this with your family or a group, say "pause" where I have it written below. After a little while, pray the next line.

Our Father, who art in heaven, (Pause)
hallowed be thy name, (Pause)
thy kingdom come, (Pause)
thy will be done on earth as it is in heaven. (Pause)
Give us this day our daily bread; (Pause)
and forgive us our trespasses (Pause)
as we forgive those who trespass against us; (Pause)
and lead us not into temptation, but deliver us from
evil. (Pause)
For thine is the kingdom and the power and the glory
forever and ever. (Pause)
Amen.

What is your favorite Christian song?
(Fourth of ten)

Christopher said his favorite Christian song is called "Above All." Do you know it? The tune goes like this . . . hmm, hmm, hmm, hmm . . . oh, I guess you can't hear my humming through the pages! Well, it's a great song written by Lenny LeBlanc and Paul Baloche. It says that Jesus Christ is greater than all of the greatest things we can imagine put together. Jesus is above all powers, above all kings, above all created things and all the ways of man is Jesus. There's no way to measure what he's worth.

It's so incredible that out Savior, who is above all things, would have had us on his mind when he went to the cross. He was rejected so we could be connected to him forever. He took the fall and thought of you and me— above all.

What a reason to sing his praise! "The one who comes from above is above all" (John 3:31).

WHAT IS YOUR FAVORITE CHRISTIAN SONG?
(FIFTH OF TEN)

When I was in the "hood," I heard someone rappin' a heavy tune. It was cool. It was deep. It was sung by Andrew. It's his favorite. It's da bomb. It's about a man he knew.

And it goes something like this: (Everyone sing!)

Jesus loves me, this I know, for the Bible tells me so.
Little ones to him belong. They are weak but he is strong.
Yes, Jesus loves me! Yes, Jesus loves me!
Yes, Jesus loves me! The Bible tells me so!

Guess what! That's not some silly little kid song. It's filled with truth. It brings hope. It has so much good news! Jesus loves us, and nothing—no nothing—can separate us from the love of God the Father in Christ Jesus our Lord (Romans 8:39).

'Rap' that news 'round your heart—it rocks!

PRAYER PONDER POINT

Sara makes many requests when she prays, but her most important reason for praying is very important. Here's a quote from Sara: "I pray a lot about my family, friends, clothing, enough money, all because I'm so thankful!"

That sounds like Philippians 4:6, which reads, "In everything, by prayer and petition, with thanksgiving, present your requests to God."

Imagine filling a box with requests to send to God. Every box of prayer we pack up to send to God's throne in heaven (in care of Jesus), should include plenty of thanks.

Talk about (or write down, below) prayer requests you have today. Along with each prayer request include a reason to be thankful. Happy Thanksgiving—every day of the year!

Prayer Request	*Reason for Thanksgiving*
_____	_____
_____	_____
_____	_____
_____	_____
_____	_____
_____	_____
_____	_____

LOL!
(Laughing Out Loud)

In the middle of the summer, you can tell if you live in a really hot place when—

(A) The birds have to use potholders to pull worms out of the ground.

(B) The temperature drops below 95, and you feel a little chilly.

(C) The swimming pool feels like a hot tub.

(D) Farmers feed their chickens crushed ice to keep them from laying boiled eggs.

Now that's hot! If you have ever lived in a place where it's hot, you know that heat can really wear you out! It's hard to have energy to play outside when it's that hot. Instead of eating sweets, you spend your time eating the sweat rolling down your face. Instead of playing tag, you kind of sag around the house. That's pretty bad.

Before David repented of a big sin in his life, he wrote about his feelings. He said he felt he had no energy—as though he was in blazing heat in the middle of the summer. His words were, "When I kept silent . . . my strength was sapped as in the heat of summer" (Psalm 32:3–4). But he said when he told God about his sin and asked forgiveness, God forgave him. He felt so much better then. His guilt was gone! His joy for living was back!

Is there something bothering you that you should confess to God or to someone else? Remember the *cool*, refreshing news of forgiveness in Jesus!

Christiana's favorite is "El-Shaddai", a song written by Michael Card and John Thompson. The song has several Hebrew names for God. (Remember, the Old Testament was first written in Hebrew.)

"El Shaddai," means God Almighty, God Almighty.

"El-Elyon na Adonia," means God Most High, O Lord.

> O Lord, God Almighty, who is like you? You are mighty, O Lord, and your faithfulness surrounds you.
>
> Psalm 89:8

The song praises God for all he is and all that his name means. He is God Almighty—ALL MIGHTY! He can do all things! And in every age, every year of your life, he will be the same. His power doesn't change. He is and always will be your Almighty God, who has saved you through his Son, Jesus, and the power of his name—El Shaddai!

WHAT IS YOUR FAVORITE CHRISTIAN SONG?
(SEVENTH OF TEN)

Rochelle has a great favorite Christian song, "I am Jesus' Little Lamb." Jesus told his disciples, "I am the Good Shepherd; I know my sheep and my sheep know me" (John 10:14). We are the sheep and lambs of Jesus, the Good Shepherd. This song is so beautiful that I'm going to write out the words and let them be today's devotion.

I am Jesus' little lamb,
Ever glad at heart I am;
For my Shepherd gently guides me,
Knows my need and well provides me,
Loves me ev'ry day the same,
Even calls me by my name.
Day by day, at home, away,
Jesus is my staff and stay,
When I hunger, Jesus feeds me,
Into pleasant pastures leads me;
When I thirst, he bids me go
Where the quiet waters flow.
Who so happy as I am,
Even now the Shepherds lamb?
And when my short life is ended,
By his angel host attended,
He shall fold me to his breast,
There within his arms to rest.

WHAT IS YOUR FAVORITE CHRISTIAN SONG?
(EIGHTH OF TEN)

Kayla said her favorite Christian song is "I am a 'C'!" because it describes a Christian. Do you know this spelling song? Many words are spelled out in the song, like "Christian," "Christ," "heart," and "live eternally." Take time right now to sing it!

Hey, you guys are good singers! D.J. is tapping all twelve of his toes and the neighbor's dog is howling at the moon!

Isn't it great to be a Christian—a follower of Christ? I hope having Christ in your heart puts a smile on your face. I hope you are following Jesus with joy like the apostle Paul, who wrote, "I am not ashamed of the gospel, because it is the power of God for the salvation of everyone who believes" (Romans 1:16).

Write down what it means to be a C-H-R-I-S-T-I-A-N.

_____

_____

_____

_____

_____

I love to visit Christian schools and help lead children in their chapel services. I've noticed that one of the songs kids love to sing loudly during chapel services is "Shine, Jesus, Shine." Katie told me this is her favorite song.

It's a song to Jesus, the Lord of light, who shines his hope on his world. It's a prayer, asking God to shine his light on each person singing it. The words ask the Holy Spirit to help our faith in Jesus grow and grow and grow! It's a song-prayer asking that the light of Jesus be sent to all the world, so everyone can know him as Savior.

> Jesus said, "I am the light of the world. Whoever follows me will never walk in darkness, but will have the light of life."
>
> JOHN 8:12

Shine, Jesus, light of the world! Shine on the world! Shine on my home! Shine on my life! And help me to reflect your light—to tell others of your love through the way I act and the

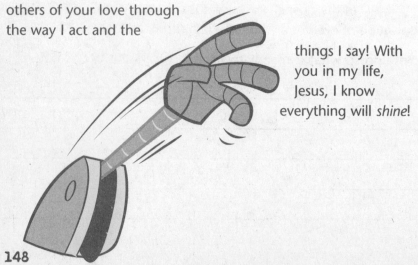

things I say! With you in my life, Jesus, I know everything will *shine*!

WHAT IS YOUR FAVORITE CHRISTIAN SONG?
(TENTH OF TEN)

Julie gets a special pass to all the rides in Great Answer Land! When asked about her favorite Christian song, she said, "I don't have one because they are all good in different ways." That's a great answer, Julie! All music that gives praise to God and worships him is good. Some are old songs; others are new. Some make you clap your hands, and others make you think quietly.

Martin Luther, who lived hundreds of years ago and wrote many Christian hymns and songs, thought music was one of the greatest gifts of God. He said, "[Music] is no invention of ours: it is a gift of God. I place it next to theology. Satan hates music: he knows how it drives the evil spirit out of us." Luther also said, "Nothing on earth is so well suited to make the heart merry, the merry sad, to give courage to the despairing, to make the proud humble, to lessen envy and hate, as music."

Wow, those are some strong words about music. But music is a great gift from God! I hope you love to sing praise to God, play songs of praise, and listen to Christian music! Some great singers and songs out there praise the Lord, just like the psalm writer, who says, "I will sing and make music to the Lord" (Psalm 27:6).

BIBLE VERSE
FILL-IN-THE-_____!

"Commit to the Lord whatever you do, and your plans will
_____."

Time to pick an answer again! (Hey, it's better than picking your nose!) What word or phrase below do you think is the right answer, according to Proverbs 16:3?

(A) Work (Alec)

(B) Go well (Crystal)

(C) Succeed (D.J.)

The answer is "C," but all four answers are pretty close. To "commit" something means to turn it over or let someone else take control of it. Commit to (turn over to) the Lord whatever you do, and your plans will succeed, prosper, go well . . . they will work!

Why do we forget to commit our God? Why don't we commit our sports teams to God? Shouldn't we commit our vacation plans to God? What about our holiday plans and friendships and families? Can you guess what will happen if we turn them over to Jesus? Hmm . . . did you forget already? They'll succeed! They'll prosper! They'll go well! They will all work out! Don't forget!

WHAT IS SOMETHING YOU THINK IS UNFAIR ABOUT GOD? (FIRST OF FOUR)

I asked kids your age this tough question. Someone told me it seems unfair that God lets bad people run around while good people die.

But guess what! Because we sin, we're all pretty bad, aren't we? We all sin, and death is the result of sin. The truth is, we will all die sometime unless we're still alive when Jesus returns to take us to heaven.

> Everyone has sinned. No one measures up to God's glory. The free gift of God's grace makes all of us right with him.
>
> ROMANS 3:23-24 (niRv)

What we need to do is make sure all people know that God has come to save them. The good news is that God isn't fair about who gets into heaven. Why is that good news? It's good because if God were really fair, none of us would go to heaven.

We are all bad—sinful. But God sent Jesus to die in our place. Whoa, that doesn't sound fair! Jesus took the punishment we deserved. And he gives sinners forgiveness and the gift of heaven. Thankfully, our salvation isn't based on how good we are!

LicKETY SPLIT
Experimental
CLEAN-UP
Vacuum
5000

WHAT IS SOMETHING THAT YOU THINK IS UNFAIR ABOUT GOD?
(SECOND OF FOUR)

Check out these words of Jesus in Matthew 5:48, "Be perfect, therefore, as your heavenly Father is perfect." Yikes! Who can be perfect? No one but Jesus. So why did he say to be perfect? One young lady I talked to at the Dr. Devo lab said, "That seems unfair!"

Wait! Don't take scissors and cut that verse out of your Bible! Think about why Jesus might have said it. First of all, Jesus expects a lot of us. Sadly, we don't expect much of ourselves. Secondly, it makes us realize that since we aren't perfect, we have to rely on Jesus and his perfect life. The only way we can be perfect is if we trust fully in Jesus to cover us. Imagine him standing in front of you, covering your life with his perfect life!

Never forget that—yes, Jesus expects us to try as hard as we can to be perfect. But also remember that we have to rely on Jesus to save us because we aren't perfect. Confused? I hope not! I hope you understand perfectly!

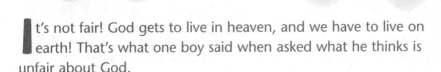

WHAT IS SOMETHING THAT YOU THINK IS UNFAIR ABOUT GOD?
(THIRD OF FOUR)

It's not fair! God gets to live in heaven, and we have to live on earth! That's what one boy said when asked what he thinks is unfair about God.

I think it's super-cool that the boy who said that is looking forward to living in heaven one day. He must know how amazing it's going to be! But while heaven is God's home, it's also our home. And God the Father sent his Son, Jesus, to make it possible for us to go home someday! We will get to spend eternity in heaven! Being in heaven will be an awesome party in honor of God, and it will never have an end!

It's not always fun living here on earth with its problems, hate, mean people, and tons of junky, pukey stuff. Jesus knows what it's like to live here on earth. But he gave the disciples hope before he left them and returned to heaven. He told them, "Do not let your hearts be troubled. Trust in God; trust also in me. I am going there to prepare a place for you. I will come back and take you to be with me." (John 14:1–3) Sounds like a fair plan to me. Thank you, Jesus, for giving us the hope of heaven!

WHAT IS SOMETHING THAT YOU THINK IS UNFAIR ABOUT GOD?
(FOURTH OF FOUR)

The best answer to this unfair question is the one several kids gave me: "There is nothing unfair about God." He's not unfair at all.

One of the best Bible stories teaching us that God is fair is the parable of the workers in the vineyard. I hope you will take time to read the story now. It's in Matthew 20:1–16. (In case you're having trouble finding it in your Bible, it's right after Matthew 19! Isn't that a great help?)

At the end of the parable (a parable, by the way, is an earthly story with a heavenly meaning), in verse 15, the landowner (who represents God) says something very important. He tells the workers (representing us), "Don't I have the right to do what I want with my own money? Or are you envious because I am generous?" The workers thought he was unfair. But he wasn't unfair at all.

Sometimes it may seem that God is unfair. He's not at all, except that that he doesn't give us the punishment we deserve because he loves us and because Jesus died for us. How awesome! Thank you! Thank you! Thank you, Jesus!

WOULD JESUS THINK A WHOOPIE CUSHION IS FUNNY? WHY OR WHY NOT?

- No. Because it's not appropriate. (James)

- Yes, because he's kind of a kid. (Caitlin)

- No, because it's making fun of his creation. (Kristin)

- Yes, because he would be glad to see us laugh! (Robert)

- No. It's a mean joke. (Kristina)

- Yes. Whoopie is fun! (Brandon)

- Of course. Everyone thinks a whoopie cushion is funny. Even girls. (Kirsten)

I also like the way Kristin thinks. She feels he would think it's funny because he's human, too, and as long as the person who sat on it thought it was funny, he would think it's funny.

I don't think Jesus wants to embarrass or upset anyone, but he does like to see us enjoying life and having fun. If you want to play a joke on someone, remember to really think about whether or not they will enjoy it. It's a matter of the heart. Remember: "A cheerful heart is good medicine, but a crushed spirit dries up the bones" (Proverbs 22:17).

So, what do you think? Would he or wouldn't he?

BIBLE VERSE
FILL-IN-THE-_____!

"As God's chosen people, holy and dearly loved, clothe yourselves with _____."

You're going to love the answer many kids gave for this one! They said "clothe yourselves with clothes!" I guess so! Cover yourself! Just like Adam and Eve did when they realized they were naked. But that's not the answer to the fill-in-the-blank according to Colossians 3:12. In an earlier devotion, we said Paul wrote that we are to clothe ourselves with the Lord Jesus Christ (Romans 13:14). But in this verse he adds more.

Check out these answers and cast your vote for your favorite. Clothe yourselves with . . .

(A) The love of Jesus (Nicholas)

(B) Joy (Taylor)

(C) Forgiveness (Tyler)

(D) The Holy Spirit (Kenny)

(E) Compassion (Paul)

The Paul in answer "E" is the apostle Paul. Do you have compassion in your closet? That's not where you'll find it! I do know someone who is giving it away though—the Holy Spirit. Just give him a call (not a phone call—a prayer call) and he'll get those to you right away! Don't worry, he delivers!

LOL!
(Laughing Out Loud)

Teacher: Billy, please make a sentence using the word "lettuce."

Billy: Please, lettuce out of school early!

Very, very funny, Billy! I decided to take the words, "let us" and put them into my special Bible computer in the Dr. Devo lab. It told me there are 143 "let us" sentences in the Bible! That's a lot of "let us"! We'd need a big salad bowl to hold them all!

Can you count all the pieces of "let-us" in Hebrews 10:24–25 (NIrv). Check it out: "Let us consider how we can stir up one another to love. Let us help one another to do good works. Let us not give up meeting together. Some are in the habit of doing this. Instead, let us cheer each other up with words of hope. Let us do it all the more as you see the day coming when Christ will return.

How many did you count? (I didn't hear your answer—speak up!) Sounds to me like we have God's recipe for a great salad here! He'll help us make it!

Let us stir up love. *Let us* do good. *Let us* help each other. *Let us* keep meeting together. *Let us* cheer each other up. *Let us* cheer each other up more and more!

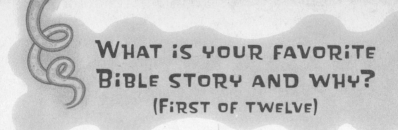

WHAT IS YOUR FAVORITE BIBLE STORY AND WHY?
(FIRST OF TWELVE)

Katherine, from Ft. Worth, Texas, told me her favorite story was about when Jesus fed more than 5,000 people. I love that story, too, Katherine! If you want to read that amazing story, it's in John 6:1–15.

Stop the presses! It's time to throw in some Dr. Devo trivia! Did you know that even though we call it the story of Jesus feeding the 5,000, Jesus really fed many, many more! Verse 10 says there were 5,000 men. That number doesn't include the women and children who were there! He could have actually fed over *10,000* people! Make that a double, Jesus!

I guess it doesn't matter if he fed just 10 people or 10,000 with 5 small loaves of barley bread and two small fish. The story shows not only the power of Jesus but also how he takes care of his people. They became hungry while he taught them. He saw their need and he dealt with it! He cares—not just about teaching us to follow him. He also cares that we are hungry! He cares about everything we need.

What needs (not wants) do you want to ask Jesus about today? Remember, miracles come in all sizes and shapes! Keep your eye out for them!

WHAT IS YOUR FAVORITE BIBLE STORY AND WHY?
(SECOND OF TWELVE)

Caitlyn told me her favorite is the story of Solomon because he made a wise decision about who was the real mother of a baby. Yes, Caitlyn, Solomon was a real wise guy! God once told Solomon he could ask for anything he wanted. (What would *you* ask for?) Solomon chose wisdom. God made him the wisest person on earth! (By the way, why does wisdom sound like it has the word "dumb" in it? Wis-dumb! Sorry, I'm just being goofy!)

1 Kings 3:16–28 is a special story that shows just how wise Solomon was. It tells of two women who each had a baby. One of the babies died, and the mother of that baby stole the other baby and said it was hers! So they brought the baby to King Solomon so that he could decide who the real mother was. The women argued and argued until wise guy Solomon asked for a sword so he could cut the baby in half and give part to each mother! I bet the women thought, "Why's the wise guy saying this?"

The real mother told Solomon not to do it! "Don't kill the baby!" she begged. But the other lady said, "Go ahead. Do it. Then neither of us will have a baby." Solomon knew that the real mother wouldn't want her baby killed, even if letting it live meant the child would be given to the other woman. So Solomon gave it to the real mother! Pretty smart, huh?

It would probably be smart of us to ask God for wisdom. Then we can all be God's wise guys . . . and girls!

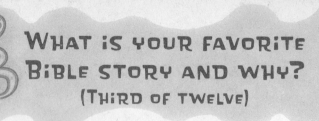

WHAT is YOUR FAVORITE BiBLE STORY AND WHY?
(THiRD OF TWELVE)

Have a friend or a family member try to figure out what Jason's favorite Bible story is. As you read it, act out the story without saying anything. You can't use words, just actions. Okay? Here's Jason's favorite. Shhhh! Don't tell anyone before you act it out! It's . . . (I'm going to whisper it, so hold the book up to your ear, please) . . . the story of Jesus' birth! Ready? Act away!

Good job of acting! You could be in the movies some day! Yes, Jason said his favorite story is Jesus' birth (you can read about it in Luke 1 and 2, as well as Matthew 2) because it's so exciting. He's right about the exciting part. That Jesus would be the Savior people had been waiting and waiting for was exciting! And the way Mary and Joseph found out about it was certainly exciting. Their trip to Bethlehem was way too exciting for Mary, who thought she'd have that baby any minute, right there on the road! Looking for a good place for his baby Jesus to be born was a little too much excitement for Joseph too!

Jesus' first bed was a manger. Then the shepherds came to visit straight from the fields! Later, some wise men also came, and King Herod ordered all children under the age of two to be killed because he didn't want Jesus to become king. Then Mary, Joseph, and Jesus had to move to Egypt to escape Herod. Whew! That's a lot of excitement! Wow!

But what is most exciting for us is that Jesus was born *for us*! He was born to bring us salvation, forgiveness for our sins, and a place in heaven. It's the most exciting truth ever!

WHAT iS YOUR FAVORITE BiBLE STORY AND WHY?
(FOURTH OF TWELVE)

I'll give you a few hints to see if you can guess Katherine's favorite Bible story.

- Hint #1—Jesus is part of the story.

- Hint #2—It's a short story.

- Hint #3—Someone in the story goes out on a limb for Jesus.

Have you figured it out? Katherine's favorite story is about Zacchaeus, the tax collector, because she likes the part where he climbs the tree. The *short* story about the *short* man is found in Luke 19:1–9. Since Zacchaeus was short, he couldn't see Jesus over the crowd. So he climbed a tree and went out on a limb to see Jesus. It paid off! Jesus saw him and said, "Zacchaeus, come down immediately. I must stay at your house today." Read the entire story to find out how Zacchaeus changed his life because of Jesus.

PSSSSST

Isn't it cool that Jesus said, "I must stay at your house today?" He *must*! Jesus wanted to stay at his house. He wanted to change Zacchaeus. Today Jesus is saying the same thing to us, through this Dr. Devo devotion: "Friend, I must stay at your house today!" Let him in! Let him in!

WHAT IS YOUR FAVORITE BIBLE STORY AND WHY?
(FIFTH OF TWELVE)

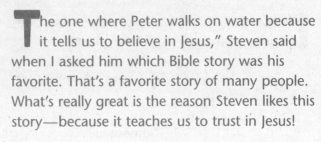

"The one where Peter walks on water because it tells us to believe in Jesus," Steven said when I asked him which Bible story was his favorite. That's a favorite story of many people. What's really great is the reason Steven likes this story—because it teaches us to trust in Jesus!

Peter knew Jesus could allow him to walk on the water, if that was Jesus' choice. Jesus invited Peter to get out of the boat and walk to him. Peter believed Jesus' invitation and trusted him. He started walking. Can you imagine? I have trouble walking very far on land without tripping! Peter was walking on water—until he stopped trusting Jesus. He took his mind off Jesus and became afraid of the wind and waves. Oops! Suddenly, Peter got a sinking feeling in his stomach because he was sinking fast! Peter cried out, "Lord, save me!"

After catching the sinking disciple, Jesus asked him, "Why did you doubt?" Jesus should ask us that question too. How would you answer him? When they got in the boat, the disciples worshiped Jesus. We can do the same thing—worship the one who forgives our doubts and strengthens our faith so we can trust in him.

Place your trust in Jesus, who has plans to take you places you never thought you'd go!

WHAT IS YOUR FAVORITE BIBLE STORY AND WHY?
(SIXTH OF TWELVE)

Okay, reader friend of Dr. Devo, here's the plan. You're going to get other people to guess Jenna's favorite Bible story. You're going to do this by drawing a picture of it. You can't make any sounds or point to anything, just draw a picture of the story and see if they can guess it. Got it? Ready? Go! Oh, I guess you need to know the story before you draw it! Here, peek! Don't let anyone see . . . It's Daniel in the lion's den. Start drawing!

Wow, you could be the next Vincent Van Gogh or—maybe not! Jenna said that story is a favorite because it's kind of scary! This story of Daniel's great trust in God and God's faithfulness is found in Daniel 6. Our main man is thrown into a locked den with lions because he continues to pray to God instead of the king. But God saves him. Those big kitty cats just purr and purr. No scratches. No nothing!

The super-cool part is that the king then said everyone in the land should worship the God of Daniel—the one true God—our God! Our God—the one who also saved *us* from certain death! That is something to roar about— and I'm not "lion!"

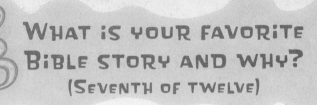
Q: Do you know why the walls in the Dr. Devo lab are always warm?

A: Because they're wearing two *coats* of paint!

That joke is so bad I should repaint, I mean, repent! I threw that coat joke in because of Quincy's favorite story. Quincy said, "It's Joseph and his coat because I like that his brothers saw their sin."

Joseph received this coat (or robe) of many colors from his father, Jacob (also known as Israel). Joseph's brothers were jealous of him. They threw him into an empty well. Then they sold him to some travelers. Jealousy isn't a very pretty thing, is it? What makes you jealous?

Quincy especially likes the story because his brothers saw their sin. In Genesis 50:15–21, the brothers ask Joseph for forgiveness but, sadly, not for the right reasons. They just don't want Joseph to pay them back for what they did. Still, Joseph tells them not to be afraid. He says, "You intended to harm me, but God intended it for good to accomplish what is now being done, the saving of many lives."

God takes things in our lives that start out bad and uses them for good. They may even save someone's life. That should make us look at bad things differently, don't you think?

Meghan's favorite story is about Paul and Silas because they looked at the bright side of things. Bright answer, Meghan!

Acts 16:16–34 tells how Paul and Silas were thrown into prison after Paul drove an evil spirit out of a woman. Both got thrown in with their feet fastened. But they made the best of the situation. They prayed and even sang hymns to God. Suddenly, there was an earthquake, and all the prison doors flew open and the chains fell right off of them. The jailer thought everyone would escape, but Paul told him not to worry. No one left.

Here's the super-cool part. The jailer wanted to know how to be saved. Paul and Silas prayed and sang to God, making the best of a bad situation, and people were saved! Not only did they baptize the jailer but his whole family believed also, and they were baptized! That whole family became believers!

Let's pray:

Forgive us, Jesus, when we forget to look at the bright side of things. We should pray and even sing when things seem bad. Use us to teach others about your love. Amen.

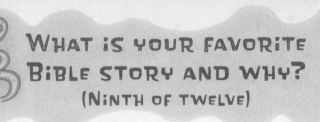

WHAT IS YOUR FAVORITE BIBLE STORY AND WHY?
(NINTH OF TWELVE)

Josh wasn't "joshin'" when he said his favorite story was the Great Commission because it tells us to witness. Some of you may not have heard of the phrase "the Great Commission," but you might know what Josh is talking about.

When someone is "commissioned," they are sent out. And the most important sending out ever was when Jesus sent his disciples (and all of his followers, including us) to take his message to all the world. This is sometimes called "the Great Commission": Jesus said, "Therefore go and make disciples of all nations, baptizing them in the name of the Father and of the Son and of the Holy Spirit, and teaching them to obey everything I have commanded you. And surely I am with you always, to the very end of the age." (Matthew 28:19–20)

Have you realized that part of your purpose on earth is to make sure others know about Jesus? It is! That's quite a responsibility. Not everyone will believe in him, but we are commissioned—sent out—to be witnesses of Jesus' love.

Think of some special ways you can do that this week. Do you know someone who doesn't believe in Jesus? Can you support some mission work in your area or in another part of the world? Whatever you do and wherever you go, remember Jesus said he will be with you always!

WHAT IS YOUR FAVORITE BIBLE STORY AND WHY?
(TENTH OF TWELVE)

Chloe told me her favorite Bible story isn't really a story, it's Psalm 91. She said, "It just kind of lets you know that God is there with you." We all need to remember that, Chloe! I think what I'll do is let D.J. type some of the verses from Psalm 91 for you while I go get my hair cut. But even though D.J. and I will be apart, we know God is with us both! Take it away, D.J.! (By the way, he types rather slowly, so just read slower! And there's one more thing—D. J. doesn't like to use periods, commas, or capital letters—except for God or Lord—so his writing might look like one long sentence. I hope you can figure it out!)

Some verses from Psalm 91 (NIrV):

The person who rests in the shadow of the most high God will be kept safe by the mighty one I will say about the Lord "he is my place of safety he is like a fort to me he is my God I trust in him he will cover you with his wings under the feathers of his wings you will find safety he is faithful he will keep you safe like a shield or a tower you won't have to be afraid of the terrors that come during the night the Lord is the one who keeps you safe so let the most high God be like a home to you the Lord will command his angels to take good care of you the Lord says "I will save the one who loves me I will keep him safe because he trusts in me he will call out to me and I will answer him I will be with him in times of trouble I will save him and honor him."

WHAT IS YOUR FAVORITE BIBLE STORY AND WHY?

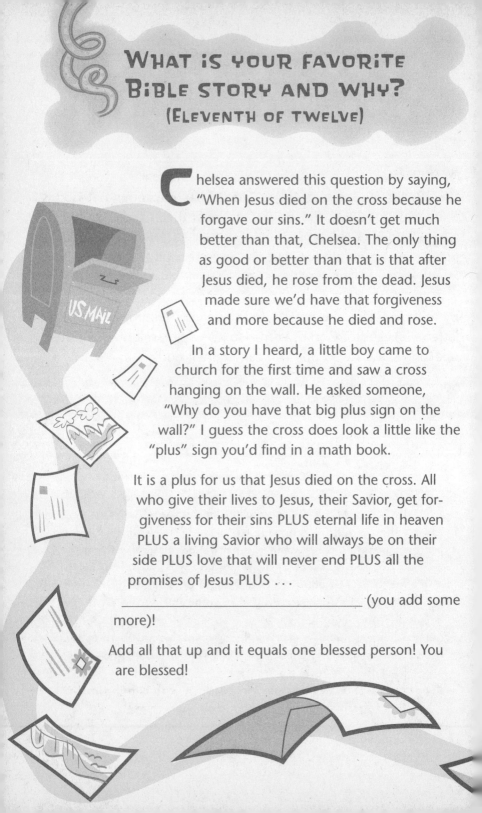

Chelsea answered this question by saying, "When Jesus died on the cross because he forgave our sins." It doesn't get much better than that, Chelsea. The only thing as good or better than that is that after Jesus died, he rose from the dead. Jesus made sure we'd have that forgiveness and more because he died and rose.

In a story I heard, a little boy came to church for the first time and saw a cross hanging on the wall. He asked someone, "Why do you have that big plus sign on the wall?" I guess the cross does look a little like the "plus" sign you'd find in a math book.

It is a plus for us that Jesus died on the cross. All who give their lives to Jesus, their Savior, get forgiveness for their sins PLUS eternal life in heaven PLUS a living Savior who will always be on their side PLUS love that will never end PLUS all the promises of Jesus PLUS . . .

_____ (you add some more)!

Add all that up and it equals one blessed person! You are blessed!

WHAT IS YOUR FAVORITE BIBLE STORY AND WHY?
(TWELFTH OF TWELVE)

Are you ready to act up again? Alexia's favorite story is a good one for you to act out as others try to guess what it is. You can't use any words. You can only act. Just in case someone else is trying to cheat by looking over your shoulder at this page, I'm going to write the answer backward! What you have to act is: yadnuS retsaE! Got it? Go ahead and act, but don't say anything!

Alexia says that's her favorite story because when she heard it she knew she would be in heaven with Jesus. That is so cool, Alexia! It's not only great to know we have a living Savior, it's also great that news makes a difference in our lives. Because Jesus lives, we too will live. Because he rose from the dead, our bodies will rise from the dead someday and join our souls, which go to heaven right away when we die. Because he lives, we live!

Here's what Paul says about it in 1 Corinthians 15:16, 20, (NIrV) "If the dead are not raised, then Christ has not been raised either. And if Christ has not been raised, your faith doesn't mean anything. Your sins have not been forgiven. But Christ really has been raised from the dead. He is the first of all those who will rise".

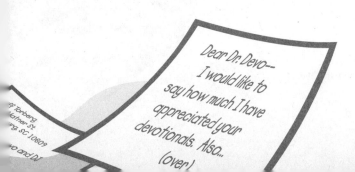

Dear Dr. Devo—
I would like to
say how much I have
appreciated your
devotionals. Also...
(over!)

4 Torberg
Mother St
rg, SC 10609
no and Di

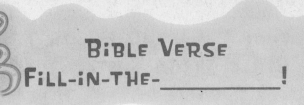

BIBLE VERSE
FILL-IN-THE-_____!

"Your attitude should be the same as that of _____."

Hey dude! Do you have an attitude? Are you sportin' a 'tude, as they say? (Who actually says that anyway?)

The Bible verse above talks about a 'tude . . . an attitude. And almost all the kids I asked to fill in the blank had the right answer—Jesus (Philippians 2:5)!

I've seen some dudes with a wild attitude and others with a tough attitude. But thankfully, I've also seen kids with an attitude like Jesus Christ. What kind of an attitude does Jesus have? Write down some words that describe Jesus' attitude.

_____   _____

_____   _____

_____

_____

_____

_____

_____

_____

_____

Those would look good
on your 'tude list too!

LOL!
(Laughing Out Loud)

Teacher: Judy, what do you call a fish with no eyes?

Judy: Fsh!

My lab assistant, D.J., doesn't get it, and my pet fish doesn't see the humor in it either. Oh well, I like it!

A verse in the Bible seems to tell us to get rid of the "I's" . . . not eyes! It says, "Don't do anything only to get ahead. Don't do it because you are proud. Instead, be free of pride. Think of others as better than yourselves (Philippians 2:3 NIrV).

Many people will tell you to watch out for yourself—for number ONE as they say. God's word says to get rid of that pride. Get rid of the I—I—I! Think about others. Things don't have to go your way. God will watch out for you. Yes, you are to care for your body and your life. But drop the selfish act. Care about others. Think of them as better than you.

What do you call a Christian without "I's?" A "chld" of God who doesn't have "prde."

PRAYER
PONDER POINT

I asked students in a Christian school to simply write a prayer. Here is Mac's prayer:

Dear Jesus, thank you for letting me go to this Christian school, and please help my grandpa get better. Amen.

Mac's prayer includes both thanksgiving and a request for help. Below are two lists. For every request you list, also name something or someone for which you're thankful. (And remember your school and family members, just as Mac did! And Dr. Devo can always use a prayer, if you have time.)

Thanksgiving: Requests:

_____   _____

_____   _____

_____   _____

_____   _____

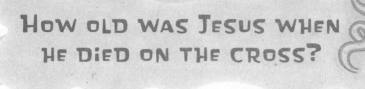

HOW OLD WAS JESUS WHEN HE DIED ON THE CROSS?

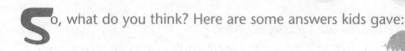

So, what do you think? Here are some answers kids gave:

- 23 years old
- 33 years old
- 49 years old
- 35 years old
- 28 years old

Well, we don't know exactly how old Jesus was when he died, but he was about 33. Luke 3:23 tells us "Jesus himself was about thirty years old when he began his ministry" and was baptized by John. We also know that his ministry was about three years long (not longer, because he was put to death).

Thirty-three may seem old to you, but really it's pretty young. Do you know anyone about that age? Maybe you haven't thought about how young Jesus was when he died. He did so much in three short years between the time he was baptized by John and his death.

What do you think God has planned for you to do in the next three years? How about the next thirty-three years? We don't know how much time we'll have on earth, but we do know our time with Jesus will never end. I pray you're never too old to enjoy hearing that good news!

WHAT DO YOU THINK THE WORD "GRACE" MEANS?

Before we ate lunch yesterday, I asked D.J. to say grace. Guess what that smarty-rodent said? You're probably right. He yelled, "GRACE!" Then he started eating. That's not what I meant! Many people call a prayer before a meal "grace." But do you know what the word "grace" means? I found several kids who knew.

Steven used each letter of the word to spell out a meaning for grace . . . like this:

> God's
>
> Riches
>
> At
>
> Christ's
>
> Expense

In other words, we get all the riches of God (forgiveness, heaven, love, hope, etc.) because Christ died! We do nothing. Christ does everything. We get the blessings!

Katherine, Tyler, and others shared a great definition of grace. It's undeserved love. That hits it right in the bulls-eye. Grace is a love that we don't deserve. So when the Bible says we are saved by grace (Ephesians 2:8), it means we are saved by God's love, which we don't deserve.

God's grace be yours!

Bible Verse
Fill-in-the-_____!

"Do not let any _____ come out of your mouths."

I won't share the name of the pre-teen who said, "Do not let any *burps* come out of your mouth." His mother would be so proud!

Here are some of the better answers:

- Bad words (Kallie)
- Lies (Nicky)
- Mean things (Dylan)

Once again, our Bible-smart Dr. Devo readers all gave great answers. The correct answer, according to Ephesians 4:29, is unwholesome talk or evil talk. But evil talk includes all the answers Kallie, Nicky, and Dylan gave.

God doesn't want us cussing, saying mean or hurtful things, saying disrespectful things, lying, or saying things that could hurt others or our relationship with him. Thankfully, God's forgiveness comes from his mouth and cleans our hearts. That love leads us to watch what we say . . . and when we burp!

LOL!
(LAUGHING OUT LOUD)

Principal: Jeremiah, why are you so late for school?

Jeremiah: I was obeying the sign on the street that says, "School ahead—Go slow!"

Do you know it's okay to be slow at school? It is! You'll even do better in school! That is, if you're slow to speak and slow to get angry. That's what James 1:19 says. Don't you think you'll also do better in school (and life) if you're quick to listen but slow to speak? You'll learn so much by listening to the advice and wisdom of others. Kids who talk a lot during class don't learn as much as those who listen. And if you get mad at others easily, your life won't be easy. So slooooooooooooow down!

Slowly read James 1:19 (NIrV): "Everyone should be quick to listen. But they should be slow to speak. They should be slow to get angry".

IF YOU COULD ASK JOHN THE BAPTIST ANY QUESTION, WHAT WOULD YOU ASK HIM?

I had my people call John's people, but he never returned my calls. I wonder why? I guess I'll answer the questions as best I can, as if I were John!

Allyson: Why did you want to be a Baptist?

John/Dr. Devo: Some of my best friends are Baptist—what's wrong with that? No, I wasn't that kind of Baptist. I was called to baptize people, to prepare their hearts for Jesus! (Mark 1:2–8)

Andrea: Why did you eat grasshoppers?

John/Dr. Devo: Because chocolate chip cookies weren't invented yet.

Kirsten: Did the locusts taste good?

John/Dr. Devo: They tasted like itty-bitty chicken fingers.

Rick: Did you get stung much when you took honey from bees?

John/Dr. Devo: Why do you think I ended up eating locusts and grasshoppers? It was much less painful!

Emiley: What was it like baptizing Jesus?

John/Dr. Devo: Humbling. Incredible. Who was I to baptize the world's Savior? He should have baptized *me*. When he was baptized heaven opened and the Spirit of God descended like a dove on him. And a voice from heaven said, "This is my Son, whom I love; with him I am well pleased."

LOL!
(Laughing Out Loud)

Q: What lives by the ocean, is grouchy, and doesn't like neighbors?

A: A hermit crab.

Is anyone out there in a grouchy mood right now? Anyone want to just get away from everything and everyone and grow up to be a hermit? Who isn't a fan of smiling today?

Everyone gets a little grouchy now and then. But, hopefully, you look forward everyday to having some fun while growing in God's love with *Dr. Devo's New-Fangled Lickety-Split Devotions!* I pray you have learned that having devotions, talking to God, and discussing your faith can be fun!

God is serious about your faith and wants you to enjoy walking with him. But he also wants to bring joy back to the lives of those

enrolled in the School of Grouchiness! He wants you to sign up for his School of Joy. And just so you know, that school's motto is Psalm 118:24: "This is the day the Lord has made; let us rejoice and be glad in it."

I hope you'll sign up today! Rejoice and be glad in this day that the Lord has made—especially for you!

WHAT DO YOU THINK IS THE WORST SIN?
(FIRST OF SIX)

Sin? Who wants to talk about sin? Yuck! But it's something we all have to deal with, so we should also talk about it in our devotions. The good news is that Jesus dealt with our sin in the perfect way, by dying on the cross and rising from the dead.

The next six devos ask about the worst sin. In a way, it's a trick question. Amy knows what I mean by that because her answer was "all of them." Tyler agreed and added this, "There is no worse sin because they are all bad." You're right, Amy and Tyler. As someone once told me, "A sin is a sin is a sin is a sin." In other words, every sin is the same in God's eyes.

Sin affects our relationship with others and with God. What we might think is a tiny little sin could end up touching many people. Have you ever stood dominoes on their ends next to each other and then tipped over the one on the end? It hits the next and makes it fall; then the next one goes down, and one by one

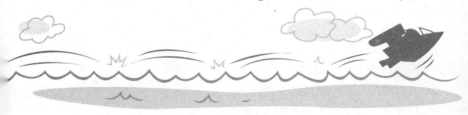

all the others do too. It's like that with sin. We tell a lie. It hurts the person to whom we lied. It can also hurt someone else.

So let's talk about sin for the next several devotions, okay? It may not be fun, but it's important. Don't worry—we're also going to talk about God's help and forgiveness! Here's a verse filled with hope, help, and forgiveness: "If you, O Lord, kept a record of sins, O Lord, who could stand? But with you there is forgiveness" (Psalm 130:3–4).

179

WHAT DO YOU THINK IS THE WORST SIN?
(SECOND OF SIX)

One answer sent in to the Dr. Devo laboratory was "loving money." Remember, we learned in yesterday's devotion that all sins are the same in God's eyes. But the pre-teen who sent this answer knew the verse from 1 Timothy 6:10, which says, "The love of money is a root of all kinds of evil. Some people, eager for money, have wandered away from the faith and pierced themselves with many griefs."

Many people think that verse says money is the root of all kinds of evil. But look closely. It doesn't say that money is the root. It says the *love of money* is the root. Lots of people have a love for money—some who have very little and some who have a lot. Gambling and lotteries are popular because so many folks have a love for money, as well as greed for more and more of it.

But what else does the verse say that is so important? (Go ahead, look and find the answer!) That's right, it says that some people, eager for money, have left the faith and brought lots of problems into their lives. That's the last thing we want to happen!

Let's pray about this: "Dear Jesus, first of all I want to praise you for who you are and for your awesome love for me and the world. If I have a love for money, please forgive me and change me. I want to have a greater love for you. I ask that all those who are having problems because they love money will turn to you for help and hope. Amen."

Shanea told the Dr. Devo interview team that her answer is worshiping other gods. That is a good answer, Shanea, because if we aren't worshiping Jesus Christ as the one true God, we won't go to heaven. No one can come to the Father, except through Jesus Christ (John 14:6).

On the other hand, we all have to admit that we put other things in front of God at times. We trust ourselves, other people, and sometimes things more than God. Are there any "other" gods in your life?

When someone asked Jesus about the greatest commandment, he said, "Love the Lord your God with all your heart and with all your soul and with all your mind" (Matthew 22:37). This means we put God above everything else in our lives, like this first commandment God gave Moses and his people says.

> Forgive me, Father, for the times that I don't put you first in my life and heart. I ask for forgiveness in Jesus' name. I know and trust that he is the only way to heaven. I give you my heart, my life, my all. I trust in your help, love, and forgiveness as I follow you.
> Amen.

WHAT DO YOU THINK IS THE WORST SIN?
(FOURTH OF SIX)

Let's take a quick quiz. Which of the following sins do you think is the worst?

    (A) Lying

    (B) Cheating on a test

    (C) Hating someone

    (D) Murdering someone

Is "D" the most popular answer? I wouldn't be surprised if it were! Obviously, murdering someone is a horrible crime. But Jesus wanted to show the people that hating others is also like murder—it's a sin. Check out 1 John 3:15! "Anyone who hates his brother is a murderer." And during his sermon on the mount, Jesus said that if you call others fools or are angry with them, you break the command that says do not murder (Matthew 5:21–24).

Jesus wants us to realize that all sins are serious. They hurt others. They hurt our own lives. They hurt our relationship with God.

Dear Lord of life, this is hard to admit and confess, but since I have been angry at others and maybe even hated someone, I am a murderer. Wow! That makes me look differently at the way I act. In my mind, I am running to your cross, asking for your forgiveness. Teach me to love as you love and forgive as you forgive. In Jesus' name. Amen.

WHAT DO YOU THINK IS THE WORST SIN?
(FIFTH OF SIX)

Someone told me they think the worst sin is hurting someone in your family. Although we said in the past devotions that no sin is any worse than another, this one can feel extra bad. That's probably because families are supposed to be about loving, not hurting. Sadly, we often hurt those who are closest to us. Hurting family members, like hurting anyone else, is a sin—whether it's their feelings, bodies, or reputations.

Another very sad thing about this sin is that it keeps family members apart. Maybe one family member won't forgive another so they don't speak to each other. Or it could be that one person isn't sorry for hurting another. God wants family members to love and forgive each other.

No family is perfect. Every family has arguments, disagreements, and problems. But God calls each family to serve and love him. He wants to teach families how to love and forgive.

Like Joshua, we can say, "as for me and my household, we will serve the Lord" (Joshua 24:15). And serving the Lord means serving our family by forgiving, just as God has forgiven us.

WHAT DO YOU THINK IS THE WORST SIN?
(SIXTH OF SIX)

We're going to close this series about sin with a teaching of Jesus that many people are confused about. One of the kids who answered this question told D.J. and me that the worst sin is not believing in Jesus. And we finally have a correct answer to this kind of tricky question!

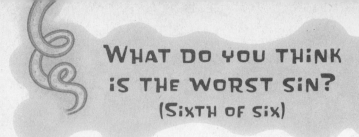

Listen to this verse from Matthew 12:32: "Anyone who speaks a word against the Son of Man will be forgiven, but anyone who speaks against the Holy Spirit will not be forgiven." Have you heard that before? Some people call it the "sin against the Holy Spirit."

Here's the problem. Many people are scared that maybe they've committed this sin and they won't be forgiven. But here's the scoop: The Holy Spirit's work is to create faith within us and keep us in that faith. So if we go against the Holy Spirit's work, we are saying we don't believe in Jesus Christ as our Savior. If we aren't believers when we die or when Christ returns, then we won't have forgiveness, and we won't have the gift of heaven. Those gifts come through faith in Jesus Christ.

But if you believe in Jesus as your Savior and place your faith in him, you have nothing to worry about. You are a forgiven child of the Heavenly Father! Heaven is yours, through Jesus! Forgiveness is yours, through your Savior. God is on your side! You are very blessed and loved!

LOL!
(Laughing Out Loud)

Can you figure out this riddle?

> A man was driving a black truck. His lights were not on. The moon was not out. A lady was crossing the street. How did the man see her?

Hmmmmmm. Give up? Don't make it harder than it is! Think about it a while if you still don't get it. I'll hang out with you. I've got all the time in the world! I'll just clip D.J.'s toenails while you think.

Okay, in case you weren't able to figure it out, the answer is: It was a BRIGHT, SUNNY DAY! Ahhh! Don't you feel silly now that you've heard how easy the answer is? You thought it must be a dark night, but the riddle never said that!

Are you walking in the light? Psalm 89:15 says, "Blessed are those . . . who walk in the light of your presence, O Lord." We know God is always with us. He's so obvious. And he says, "Come, walk with me."

Are you having a dark day or maybe not feeling too smart? Don't make life harder than it is. Walk with Jesus, the Light of the World. The answer to all your worry is easy. It's Jesus!

ANOTHER
LIGHT SUBJECT

Someone sent me an email with a letter to God in it. It cracked me up, so I thought I'd share it with you, even though I didn't interview this young girl.

> Dear God,
> In school we read that Thomas Edison made light, but in Sunday School they said you did it first. Did he steal your idea?
> Sincerely, Donna

Thomas Edison would have been shocked to hear someone thought he stole light from God! But God did help him invent the electric light.

Is it possible to steal from God? Actually, it is—but not light! Malachi 3:8 (NIrV) says one way we can steal from him. [The Lord says,] "Will a man dare to steal from me? But you rob me! You ask, 'How do we rob you?' By holding back your offerings."

Wow, I guess God's Word can shed some light on the subject of giving offerings for his kingdom! Thomas may not have stolen God's light, but I'm glad Jesus has stolen our hearts with his great, forgiving love, as we learn to give to him joyfully.

PRAYER PONDER POINT

Listen to and pray this prayer that Kellie wrote:

> Dear Jesus,
> Please help me get over my fears and
> help me understand your Word.
> Amen.

Kellie had two requests: (1) that God would help her get over her fears and (2) that he would help her understand his Word. I think Kellie will get over her fears as God, the Holy Spirit, helps her understand his Word.

God's Word, the Bible, helps us get over our fears. From it, we learn to trust God in all things. In it, he shares stories of how he has helped others who were once afraid. The Bible is filled with promises that will zap our fears and help us live peacefully.

> I have chosen you. I have not turned my back on you. So do not be afraid. I am with you. Do not be terrified. I am your God. I will make you strong and help you. My powerful right hand will take good care of you. I always do what is right.
>
> Isaiah 41:9–10 nirv

As you pray, always remember to ask the Holy Spirit to help you understand his Word. It will make all the difference in your words.

WHERE DID JESUS LIVE WHEN HE WAS GROWING UP?

Here are some of the answers I received for this question:

- Nazareth (Kelly)
- Judah (Kaitlyn)
- Bethlehem (Lindsey)
- Jerusalem (Karrah)
- Galilee (Shane)
- Israel (Trenton)
- Egypt (Matthew)

You're right! Jesus may not have had a home in all these places, but he was in all these places while growing up. Some of the places are areas or countries; some are towns. If your Bible has a map, maybe you and your family or class can look them up.

The reason I asked this question is because I know a lot of you have either moved around a lot or have family or friends who do. Moving from place to place can be hard on kids, friends, and even family members.

When Joshua had to take over leading God's people and moving them into the Promised Land, the Lord told him, "As I was with Moses, so I will be with you; I will never leave you or forsake you" (Joshua 1:5).

Are you sad about a move? Remember that as the Lord was with Moses and Joshua as they moved, so he will be with you. He will never leave you nor forsake you!

IF YOU WERE ASKED TO WRITE SOMETHING TO PUT IN THE BIBLE, WHAT WOULD YOU ADD?

Jason responded, "I would write the meanings for some of the words." The Bible does use some words we don't use very often. We may not understand what they mean.

Luke 24:13–35 is the story of Jesus and two men on the road to Emmaus. Jesus explains to the men what was said about him in Scripture. They didn't understand it all. They needed help.

To help you with words you don't understand, here's a very little Dr. Devo Big Bible Words Definition List.

- **Atonement**: By his death, Jesus *atoned* or made up for our sins. He paid the penalty for us.

- **Justification**: To *justify* means to declare "not guilty." Our justification occurred when Jesus died on the cross in our place. That gift came to life for us when the Holy Spirit created faith in us. Through faith in Jesus, we are declared "not guilty" before the Father, because Jesus stands in our place.

- **Redemption**: God's act of *buying back* sinful humans. Jesus bought us back from sin and death. He gave his life to redeem us.

- **Sanctification**: To *sanctify* means to make holy. The Holy Spirit sanctifies us. As Christians, we are living the sanctified life.

Whew! Big words with important meanings from a big God!

Bible Verse
Fill-in-the-_____!

"Train a child in the way he should go and when he is old he will not _____."

L adies and gentlemen, boys and girls, here are your choices to fill in the blank above. Take your best pick!

(A) Go the opposite way of heaven (Jane)

(B) Believe in false gods (Allison)

(C) Be in jail (Rachel)

(D) Stop believing (Alissa)

(E) Turn from it (Solomon)

If you didn't figure it out, the first four are real kids, and the Solomon in answer "E" was a king—a very wise one who wrote those words in Proverbs 22:6.

Solomon knew that if parents would raise their children in God's way, teaching them to love the Lord with all their hearts and to serve God and others with joy, it will make a big difference when they are older.

You know what I think, gang. If you have Christian parents who care deeply about your faith, make sure you thank them—over and over again!

IF JESUS WOULD TELL YOUR PARENTS ONE THING ABOUT YOU, WHAT WOULD YOU WANT HIM TO SAY? (FIRST OF SIX)

Put on your imagination hats! Jesus walks into your house (he knocks first) and says he'd like to talk to your parents—about you! When I asked Kelly what she thinks Jesus would say to her parents, she answered, "Good things!" We'd all hope for that!

Jesus knows everything we do, say, and think. The real miracle is that he still loves us! And because he loves us, he does have good things to say about us.

Zephaniah 3:17 says, "The Lord your God . . . will take great delight in you . . . he will rejoice over you with singing."

Tell your parents or guardian that the Lord takes great delight in their children . . . and in them!

IF JESUS WOULD TELL YOUR PARENTS ONE THING ABOUT YOU, WHAT WOULD YOU WANT HIM TO SAY? (SECOND OF SIX)

If Jesus talked to Amy's parents, she thinks he would say, "Amy has stood up for my name many times, and I think she will forever!" Wouldn't that be a wonderful thing for Jesus to say about us?

In the book of Revelation, Jesus encouraged the church members in Ephesus by telling them, "You have persevered for my name, and have not grown weary" (Revelation 2:3). We are called to stand up for Jesus and his ways. Most people in the world won't be very happy with us for doing it, but all heaven rejoices over those who do.

Christians in many countries, at this very moment, are being hurt or even killed because they believe in Jesus. Will you pray for those people? Will you pray that the Holy Spirit will strengthen your faith so you will always stand up for Jesus' name?

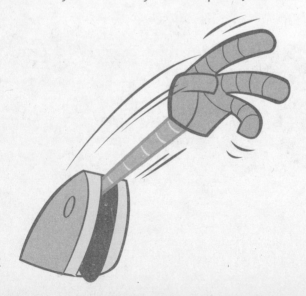

IF JESUS WOULD TELL YOUR PARENTS ONE THING ABOUT YOU, WHAT WOULD YOU WANT HIM TO SAY? (THIRD OF SIX)

Tyler and Steven had the same answers, and I'm sure the parents of each will like it! They hoped Jesus would tell their parents, "You're raising your son well." I'm sure you'll both grow up to be wonderful men of God, Tyler and Steven. And you'll have your parents and your Savior (along with others) to thank for that!

I'm sure Jesus' mother, Mary, and his stepfather, Joseph, were happy when many people told them they were raising their son well. After all, he was the perfect son! But I like what Luke 2:52 (NIrV) says about Jesus growing up. It's something that you can pray for, even if you're not the perfect son or daughter!

The verse says, "Jesus became wiser and stronger. He also became more and more pleasing to God and to people."

IF JESUS WOULD TELL YOUR PARENTS ONE THING ABOUT YOU, WHAT WOULD YOU WANT HIM TO SAY? (FOURTH OF SIX)

Jenna's prayer is that Jesus would tell them that all her family members would be in heaven. Does all your family believe in Jesus as their Savior? What about aunts and uncles, grandparents and cousins?

When the Christian church was just a baby, Acts 2:42–47 says that families got together to pray and learn from God's teachings. They would care for each other and make sure everyone had what they needed. When families get together to do those things, they not only grow in love for each other, they also grow in their love for God. Those verses end with this great news about the families of believers: "And the Lord added to their number daily those who were being saved."

Dear Lord, add daily to the number being saved in our families, neighborhoods, schools, towns, cities, and nations. Save, Jesus, save! Amen.

IF JESUS WOULD TELL YOUR PARENTS ONE THING ABOUT YOU, WHAT WOULD YOU WANT HIM TO SAY? (FIFTH OF SIX)

Aaron gets an "A" on the answer he gave for this question! Picture Jesus walking up to your mom or dad. He puts his hands on their shoulders and looks them right in the eyes. With a little smile he says, "Your son will get 'A's' in the future!" That's what Aaron wants!

Maybe Aaron gave that answer right after report cards came out, and there wasn't an "A" to be found. Or maybe he had recently promised his parents he would do better in school. It would be nice to get an "A" in every subject in every class we ever take. Most likely that won't happen. But Aaron didn't ask for that. He just asked that there would be some "A's" in the future.

That's great of Aaron to make a commitment to do better. He wants to work harder and get better grades. I'm sure not only will his parents be pleased with that but he will also.

The book of Proverbs is filled with many wise words about either being lazy or working hard. These words might have something to say about school work, chores around the house, or your job when you're older. One verse that comes to mind is, "Hands that don't want to work make you poor. But hands that work hard bring wealth to you" (Proverbs 10:4 NIrV).

Lord, take my hands, mind, and body. Use them wisely and for your glory. Amen.

One answer almost broke my heart. A girl wanted Jesus to tell her parents: "Sometimes your daughter feels very sad." That makes me sad. And it makes Jesus sad too.

First, my advice to this girl and any of you who feel sad a lot is to tell a parent or another adult you trust—maybe a relative, teacher, pastor, or family friend. Second, keep talking to God about it and hear his words of love for you.

The Bible contains many stories of people going through sad times. Some are in the Psalms. Another story is about Elijah, who had a rough time for a while. You can read about it in 1 Kings 19. Elijah is exhausted and depressed. He even wants to die. He falls asleep, and the Lord sends an angel to care for him. The angel brings him food and drink. With God's help, Elijah is able to keep going. Later God speaks to him and gives him hope. Elijah is a dearly loved man of God. And by the way, you—yes, YOU—are a dearly loved, forgiven child of God! Don't give up! Look up and see ways Jesus is sending you help for your sad times!

BiBLE VERSE
FiLL-iN-THE-_____!

"There is a time for everything . . . a time to _____ and a time to _____."

Some answers I received were:

- Sing . . . praise (Christopher)
- Live . . . die (Lyn)
- Plow . . . fight (Joel)

Ecclesiastes 3:1–8 gives lots of answers to this one. Use that passage (it's below) for your devotion today. Then answer this question: What is it time for right now in your life?

"There is a time for everything, and a season
for every activity under heaven:
a time to be born and a time to die, a time
to plant and a time to uproot,
a time to kill and a time to heal, a time to
tear down and a time to build,
a time to weep and a time to laugh, a time
to mourn and a time to dance,
a time to scatter stones and a time to
gather them, a time to embrace
and a time to refrain,
a time to search and a time to give up, a
time to keep and a time to throw away,
a time to tear and a time to mend, a time
to be silent and a time to speak,
a time to love and a time to hate, a time
for war and a time for peace."
ECCLESIASTES 3:1–8

PRAYER PONDER POINT

Ashley wrote a beautiful prayer to her Savior:

> Dear Jesus,
> Thank you for giving and forgiving.
> Amen.

For this Prayer Ponder Point, use that prayer to fill-in-the-blanks below with your prayer requests.

Thank you for giving me
_____.

Thank you for forgiving me my sin of
_____.

Thank you for giving me
_____.

Thank you for forgiving me my sin of
_____.

Thank you for giving me
_____.

Thank you for forgiving me my sin of
_____.

In Jesus's name.
Amen.

Lord, be merciful to me
and hear my prayer.
PSALM 4:1

WHAT'S THE BEST THING ABOUT YOUR BEST FRIEND?

Sara wrote this about her friends: "I have a lot of good friends, but there are a few very close ones. I love that I can tell them anything and they understand."

Friends are understanding! We can tell them anything. They care and understand. Hey, that sounds just like our Savior! It's great if we have friends that imitate the friendship of Jesus! Thank him (and them) for that! Our God calls us his friends and, as Psalm 147:5 says, God is great, his power is mighty, and there is no limit to his understanding.

- Are you an understanding friend?

- Do your friends find it easy to tell you things?

- How can you be a better friend?

- How can you thank your friends for being there for you and understanding?

- Who wants to teach you how to be a better friend? (The answer to that one, my friends, in case you don't know, starts with the letter "J" and ends in "esus!")

By the way, have I ever told you that I'm glad you are my friend! Well, I want you to know that I thank God for you!

APPROXIMATELY HOW MANY PEOPLE DO YOU KNOW THAT BELIEVE IN JESUS AS THEIR PERSONAL SAVIOR?

How many do you know? My Dr. Devo interview answers varied from a lot to a little, like this:

- A great number
- About 400
- About 25
- About 20
- About 100
- Everyone I know

I will praise you, O Lord, with all my heart; I will tell of all your wonders!

PSALM 9:1

Here's what we're going to do first—stand up (go ahead, don't be shy)! Let's give the Holy Spirit a standing ovation for saving all those people! Clap! Shout! Praise! (Okay, you can sit down. Thanks for putting up with me!)

Now, let's think about some of the believers whose faith has made a big difference in our lives. Of the people on your list, which ones know Jesus as their Savior and regularly tells you about Jesus? Which ones have really strong faith? What have you learned from the faithful people around you? I think it would be a great idea to thank them, don't you? I hope you'll take the time to tell them, write them, call them, email them—whatever you want! They are gifts to you from God!

Last, let's thank God for his people in our lives who are our faith heroes and helpers!

APPROXIMATELY HOW MANY PEOPLE DO YOU KNOW THAT DO NOT BELIEVE IN JESUS AS THEIR PERSONAL SAVIOR?

Most people said there weren't many people they knew that didn't believe in Jesus as their personal Savior. I have a feeling there are many more than we know! The Bible tells us that "many are invited but few are chosen" when it comes to heaven. These are some of the answers I received.

- Not as many as ten
- About 200
- Lots
- About 50
- I don't really know of any

There are more people in the world who don't know Jesus as their Savior than there are those who do trust and believe in him. I found it interesting that the biggest numbers in answer to both this question and the last devotion question came from Louisa, who lives in Russia. She said she knew about 400 people who did know Jesus as their Savior and about 200 who didn't. No matter what country we live in, we need to get the word out about Jesus and his love. It's a matter of life and death.

You may want to use Psalm 67:1–2 for your prayer as you live as a missionary in your neck of the woods—wherever that is. Those prayer-words are, "May God be gracious to us and bless us and make his face shine upon us, that your ways may be known on earth, your salvation among all nations."

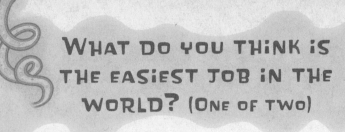

Warning! Warning! If your relatives have any of these jobs, be ready to calm them down!

- Sam votes for a mail carrier. (You may get letters disagreeing with you, Sam!)

- Emiley says cutting hair. (I wouldn't tell that to the person who cuts your hair, Emiley!)

- Jordan thinks working at a fast food restaurant is the easiest. (I'd watch what those cooks put in your food next time, Jordan.)

- Jackie told me being a model is easiest because all you have to do is smile, walk, and wear cute clothes. You don't even have to fix your own make-up or hair! (No comment from Dr. Devo!)

- Abby is living on the edge because she thinks the easiest job is being a stay-at-home mom!

- Amanda figures there is no easiest job because every person has a race to run, and although it may look easy, it is not.

Okay, some jobs may be easier than others, but no job is just plain easy, if you're doing it to the best of your God-given ability. Did you know that hard work came with sin? Yep. The Lord told Adam that in Genesis 3:17–19. And Amanda has some good advice—don't judge the jobs of others. Give thanks to God for your life, your calling, and whatever you are asked to do—then do it so God gets the glory, not you! That's not always the easiest thing to do either!

WHAT DO YOU THINK IS THE EASIEST JOB IN THE WORLD? (Two of two)

I had to add another devotion with this question because I received several answers that aren't really jobs but kids gave them anyway. They made me think. Anyway, here are those extra answers to the question, "What do you think is the easiest job in the world?"

- Wiping the table after supper
- Praying
- Sitting at home watching TV
- Jumping
- Taking out the trash
- Going to the bathroom

The point in adding these (except for that last one) is that whether you clean the table, pray, sit at home, jump, take out the trash, or whatever—you should do it all for the glory of God. In fact, that's what 1 Corinthians 10:31 tells us. It reads, "So whether you eat or drink or whatever you do, do it all for the glory of God."

Maybe you want to make a sign to put in your room with the words, "All for the glory of God!" to help you remember these wise words Paul wrote.

TRICK QUESTION!

When I sent out some questions to kids, I had a trick question on the list. I know that wasn't very nice. The question I asked was, "Who was in the fiery furnace with Daniel?" I added that spelling doesn't matter. What was tricky about it was that Daniel wasn't in the fiery furnace. But that story is in the book of Daniel. And the ones in the furnace were Daniel's friends—Shadrach, Meshach, and Abednego. (That's why I said spelling wouldn't count. And, wow, did I get some interesting ways to spell their names!)

Kyle and a couple others knew Daniel wasn't in the fiery furnace! Several others left it blank, so maybe the question tricked them!

Being tricked isn't always fun, is it? I think King Nebuchadnezzar (try spelling that one) felt like he had been tricked when he had Shadrach, Meshach, and Abednego put in the blazing furnace. The king threw them in because they wouldn't bow down to a gold idol the king had made. It was ninety-feet high and nine feet wide! But God made sure the three men who believed in the true God and only worshiped him wouldn't be harmed. Sure enough, they weren't burned at all! God used that miracle so that the king would let others worship the true God! Pretty tricky, huh?

IF YOU COULD ASK THE DISCIPLE MATTHEW ANY QUESTION, WHAT WOULD YOU ASK?

Sydney would like to ask Matthew if she could take writing lessons from him—the author of the first book in the New Testament!

Check out these other great answers:

- Mark: How he felt when he met Jesus.

- Abby: Was it cool hanging with Jesus?

- Sue: What was it like when you heard that Jesus wanted you to be his disciple?

- Louisa: What led you to just get up and follow Jesus when he told you to leave your collecting table and follow him?

Since we're disciples (followers of Jesus), like Matthew, answer the same questions as if Matthew were asking you!

- How did you feel when you first met Jesus?

- What's cool about hanging with Jesus?

- What was it like when you heard Jesus wanted you to be his disciple?

- What led you to just get up and follow Jesus?

Here's a good Bible verse for all disciples to think about today: "Always be ready to give an answer to anyone who asks you about the hope you have. Be ready to give the reason for it" (1 Peter 3:15).

HOW MANY BOOKS ARE THERE IN THE BIBLE?

Here are some of the answers kids gave:

- 25
- 35
- 42

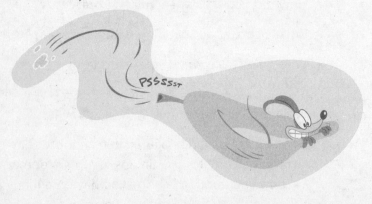

- 66
- 81
- 100

Which do you think is correct?

Here's a trick to help you remember how many books are in the Old Testament. The word "Old" has three letters, and the word "Testament" has nine. Put the three and nine next to each other and you have 39. There are 39 books in the Old Testament.

The word "New" also has three letters, and "Testament" has nine. If you multiply 3 x 9, you get 27. There are 27 books in the New Testament.

Now you can add 39 + 27 to find out how many books are in the Bible! And remember that the Word of God is living and active (Hebrews 4:12).

PSSSSsт

What's the most important thing you've learned in Sunday school?

Katie didn't need to dig deep in Dr. Devo's laboratory of great answers to figure this out. She said, "That God loves us!"

It sounds so simple, doesn't it? Having someone love us is a terrific thing! It's a great feeling. Being loved can even change the way we do things. It can cause smiles to break out on our faces and tingly bumps to run up and down our backs.

But knowing Jesus loves us is more than a great feeling. It's a zillion times better than the love of other people. Jesus' love will never change. His love comes with a promise to always be with us. His love changes the way we can love others.

> May the grace shown by the Lord Jesus Christ, and the love that God has given us, and the sharing of life brought about by the Holy Spirit be with you all.
>
> 2 Corinthians 13:14 NIRV

Give thanks today for your Sunday school's teachers, helpers, and leaders who teach kids like you that Jesus loves them! It can change the world!

LOL!
(Laughing Out Loud)

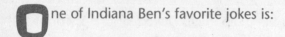

One of Indiana Ben's favorite jokes is:

Q: What do you call a flying skunk?

A: A smellicopter!

Here's one of Bethany's giggle questions:

Q: Why do giraffes have long necks?

A: Have you ever smelled a giraffe's feet?

D.J. is wondering if you think those jokes stink, while I'm on the scent of a sweet smelling verse in the Bible. Aha! I found it—2 Corinthians 2:15 (NIrV)! Paul writes, "God considers us to be the sweet smell that Christ is spreading among people who are being saved and people who are dying. To the one, we are the smell of death. To the other, we are the perfume of life."

Let me help you understand what this means. Imagine walking into your kitchen. You smell the sweet scent of brownies, cookies, or another of your favorite desserts. (I wish this was a "Scratch and Sniff" book!) Come closer to get a better smell. Mmmm!

Paul says the good news of Jesus we share is a sweet smell people are drawn to. See, that news doesn't stink at all! Go smell up the neighborhood—you sweet-smelling thing, you!

Yet Another Question for Mary

If Sara were a reporter at a news conference, she would ask Mary, "Were you ever liked or disliked just because Jesus was your son?"

Has someone liked you just because of something you had or because you hung out with a certain group? Or maybe they disliked you because of who you are, where you live, or what you look like.

I'm sure Mary could relate. It wasn't easy being Jesus' mother. People in her day were the same as people today. We're all sinners who sometimes like or dislike people for the wrong reason. We need to be glad Jesus forgives us for those times and helps us care about others in the right way—his way!

If you have problems with others liking you or not liking you for the wrong reasons, remember to keep your heart focused on God's ways. The psalm writer shares some fitting words: "Many enemies attack me. But I haven't turned away from your covenant laws" (Psalm 119:157 NIrV).

WILL WE GO TO THE BATHROOM IN HEAVEN? WHY, OR WHY NOT?

This is a toughie because the Bible talks about food and drink in heaven but doesn't say what our heavenly bodies will do with it. Deborah thinks going to the bathroom started when sin came into the world with Adam and Eve. Hmmmm. Sarah thinks a bathroom in heaven would be very nice. And several had a similar thought: "Yes, because you got to go sometime!"

D.J.'s favorite answer came from Henry: "No, because it would go through the clouds."

What do you think? I know we won't be hungry or thirsty, hurting or sad (Revelation 7:16–17).

Here's my expert opinion—I don't know if we'll go to the bathroom in heaven and it doesn't matter! No matter what the real answer is, the important thing is that we're heading to heaven because of our faith in Jesus and what he has done for us!

Bible Verse
Fill-in-the-_____!

"I will sing praise to my God as long as _____."

It's time to put your Bible knowledge to use. Did Kristine, Luke, or Barrett give the right answer, according to both Psalm 104:33 and Psalm 146:2? If you don't know for sure, you'll have to put your "guess knowledge" to use!

      (A) I want (Kristine)

      (B) forever (Luke)

      (C) I live (Barrett)

Could someone please provide a drum roll? Thank you. Barrett (answer "C") is correct. I will sing praise to my God as long as I live. That's the right answer according to the Psalms. But if you want to debate the answer, you could say it's "B!" Why? Because we're not going to stop singing praise to God while we live on earth. We'll sing his praise forever, including in heaven. On the other hand, if we will be living both on earth and in heaven, that means "C" is right again. Ohhhhh! I'm so confused!

Let's get unconfused! Here's what matters— sing praise to God while you live every day . . . on earth and then in heaven, forever! Amen to that!

Prayer
Ponder Point

Who do you pray for the most, and why?

Matt told the Dr. Devo interview team that he prays for his great grandma the most because she's almost 100 years old. That's almost as old as some of the food in D.J.'s miniature refrigerator!

Matt has given me a good idea for this Prayer Ponder Point. We probably forget to pray often enough for people who are older. (Even older than your parents!) Grandparents and great-grandparents (and many who don't have children or grandchildren) have special needs and prayer requests.

Often those needs are about health. Sometimes the elderly don't have enough money to pay the bills. They may be lonely. Some don't know Jesus. There are so many reasons to pray for older people and so many things to pray about. Read Jude 1:20–21, make a prayer list for older people you know, and then lift them up to God in prayer!

_____

_____

_____

_____

_____

_____

WHAT DOES "HALLELUJAH" MEAN?

Here are the possible answers. Which one do you think is correct?

   (A) Happy! (Tom)

   (B) God is great! (Lauren)

   (C) Praise the Lord! (D.J.)

   (D) Yippie! (Mark)

If you guessed, "C", be happy and shout "Yippie!" Yes, God is great, so praise the Lord! Hallelujah, also spelled "Alleluia," means "Praise the Lord!"

> Praise the Lord.
> Praise the Lord,
> O my soul.
> PSALM 146:1

Here's a little Hebrew lesson for you. "Hallel" in the Hebrew language means "praise." And the "jah" or "yah" part of the word is short for "Yahweh," which is the personal name of the Lord.

The next time you sing hallelujah or alleluia in a song or hymn, remember you're saying, "Praise the Lord!" When you think about how blessed you are (and you are *very* blessed) shout out—in your mind or out loud—Hallelujah! Alleluia! Praise the Lord! Or the next time you read the words, "Praise the Lord" in the Bible, you can remember that in Hebrew, the word is "Hallelujah!"

WHAT DOES THE BIBLE MEAN WHEN IT SAYS THAT OUR BODIES ARE THE TEMPLE OF THE HOLY SPIRIT?

Does the Bible really say that? My Dr. Devo body looks more like a stadium than a temple! Joel told me that when Paul wrote those words, he meant that our bodies are precious, and we should treat them well. Sounds like you're right on target, Joel!

Here's what Paul writes in 1 Corinthians 6:19–20: "Do you not know that your body is a temple of the Holy Spirit, who is in you, whom you have received from God? You are not your own; you were bought at a price. Therefore honor God with your body."

Guess what? You get to write the rest of this devotion by answering the following questions and then ending in prayer! How's that for a deal? May the Holy Spirit bless your discussion!

1. How is the Holy Spirit in us?

2. How did we receive the Holy Spirit?

3. What does Paul mean by saying, "You are not your own?"

4. At what price were you bought?

5. Who bought you?

6. How do you plan to honor God with your body?

WHAT DOES YOUR FIRST NAME MEAN?

Christine said her name means "Christian," and Christopher told me his means "Christ-bearer." I don't know if these are correct, but I do hope Allison isn't lying because she said her name means "Truthful!" Here are other answers:

- Sarah—princess
- Ally—I don't know but everyone calls me Allyoop!
- Ross—Red Rose
- Benjamin—son of my right hand
- James—follower of Jesus

The Bible contains so many names for God—Father, Son, and Holy Spirit. The meaning of each name tells a little story about who God is and what he is about. Use these different names as you pray:

- "Jesus" means "the one who saves" (Savior!) (Read Matthew 1:21).
- "Christ" means "Anointed One" (Messiah).
- "Immanuel" means "God with us" (Check out Matthew 1:23).
- "Rabbi" is the word for "teacher" or "my great one."
- "Alpha and Omega" are the first and last letters of the Greek alphabet. Jesus is the first and the last, the beginning and the end (Revelation 1:8).

DO YOU THINK EVERYONE WHO WEARS "CROSS" JEWELRY KNOWS WHAT THE CROSS MEANS?

Almost everyone I asked said they don't think everyone who wears a cross knows its meaning. Some kids added that it just looks cool. Others said, "It's what everyone wears, so they wear it."

Sadly, I think the kids who gave me those answers are correct. I would guess it makes Jesus sad to see people who don't care about the cross wearing this symbol that tells so much about him.

We shouldn't wear a cross because we think it looks good to God or others. It doesn't have special powers either. The power isn't in the cross; it's in Jesus. The cross can be a reminder to us and others that Jesus died on the cross for all people. It may bring comfort when we see it or hold it in our hands, remembering how much Jesus loved us—enough to die so we can live.

I like what Paul said about the importance of what happened on the cross. If you wear a cross, maybe you can think about these words when you put on your cross: "We preach Christ crucified" (1 Corinthians 1:23). Those words aren't just for preachers. We should all proclaim Christ crucified and the living Christ in all we do and say. Thankfully, the Holy Spirit helps us in that calling.

LOL!
(Laughing Out Loud)

A pre-teen boy said the prayer at family dinner one night. "Dear God, thank you for these pancakes." When the prayer was over, his parents asked him why he thanked God for pancakes when they were having chicken. He smiled and said, "I thought I'd see if He was paying attention."

Do you ever feel that God isn't paying attention to you? At times like that you might feel like screaming, "Hey God! I'm over here! I need your help! Pay attention to me! Where are you? I don't know if you care about what I have to say! Yo! Yoohoo! Hey, hey, hey! Pay attention, God! Pleeeeaaassseee!

We may feel like that sometimes, but we know God always keeps his promises. He has told us he will never leave us or forsake us and that he knows all our thoughts and words. Never doubt that.

When King Solomon dedicated the temple to the Lord, part of his prayer was that God would pay attention to all the prayers of his people. Solomon's prayer wasn't exactly like the boy's prayer of thanks for the pancakes, but he did say, "My God, let your eyes see us. Let your ears pay attention to the prayers that are offered in this place" (2 Chronicles 6:40).

Does the Old Testament have anything in it about Jesus?

The answers to this question were about equally divided between yes and no. Two girls had great thoughts to share.

Kirsten said, "OF COURSE! The prophesies tell that God will send his Son, and everyone should wait for Him to come. Besides, God and Jesus are the same person, and God is present in the Old Testament so Jesus is also there because he is God."

And Jackie responded, "Yes, a lot of prophets told that a Savior would be coming. When the people put the blood of the lamb on the doorway so that the death angel would pass over their houses, it was kind of like Jesus (the Lamb of God) dying on the cross (giving his blood) to save us from our sin and death."

Wow! Great help, girls! Everything in the Old Testament points toward Jesus! It's all about him—in the Bible and in our lives!

WHAT IS A PROPHET?

- Abby told me a prophet is "someone who hears from God—a lot!"

- Amanda answered, "A person who tells people about God and is a big follower of God.

- Jordan said a prophet is "someone who writes the word of God."

- Daniel feels it's "someone God chose to send messages to other people."

- And Louisa shared, "A person who God reveals facts or the future to or tells what is going to happen. The prophet then tells these messages from God to other people."

You're all right! Prophets can be described in many different ways. Some have books named after them in the Old Testament, telling God's story through their lives. God chose prophets (like Daniel noted) to tell others about his word. Often, as Abby said, God spoke to them in some way—often about what would happen in the future, like Louisa shared. Then this follower of God would tell people about God and his messages—so you're right, Amanda!

HOW MANY OLD TESTAMENT BOOKS NAMED AFTER PROPHETS CAN YOU LIST? HERE'S MY LIST!

Books named for prophets: Isaiah, Jeremiah, Ezekiel, Daniel, Hosea, Joel, Amos, Obadiah, Jonah, Micah, Nahum, Habakkuk, Zephaniah, Haggai, Zechariah, Malachi.

WHAT DOES THE CHRISTIAN SYMBOL OF THE FISH STAND FOR?

Have you seen the outline of a fish stuck on the back of a car? Have you ever wondered what it stands for? David might have thought his idea sounded fishy, but he said it shows someone is Christian. It's about that easy, David!

Here's the scoop behind the meaning. It goes waaaaaaaaaay back in history—it's even older than your parents! It goes back to when the Christian church began. At that time, many Christians were killed or persecuted (hurt) because of their faith in Jesus Christ.

When Christians were talking with a person whom they didn't know well, it was a common practice to draw the sign of a fish in the sand with their sandals or write out the Greek word for fish, which was "IXIOS." (That's pronounced something like "Ick-thus.") If the person recognized the symbol, they would know that person was also a follower of Christ and they could speak freely. Each Greek letter in the word for fish stands for a name of Christ. Their letters were different than ours and they didn't look exactly like ours, but it went like this:

I-Jesus   *X-Christ*   *I-God*
O-Son   *S-Savior*

So today, when you see someone wearing the symbol of a fish or see it on a car—wherever—you can know that person is a Christian. (Unless, I guess, they just bought the car from a Christian and haven't taken the sticker off yet!) That's the story! It's all about Jesus Christ, God, Son, and Savior! There's nothing fishy about that!

WHAT'S THE SADDEST THING THAT HAS EVER HAPPENED TO YOU? (ONE OF THREE)

This group of children shared some very sad things from their lives. Each had someone close to them who died. For Kyle, it was his dad. Christine had a friend who died. Both Brittany's grandma and grandpa died. And Jordan's third base coach died of cancer. Dealing with death isn't easy, no matter how old you are and no matter who died.

Kyle, I hope you find good news in the fact that you have been blessed with a heavenly Father who will never leave you. He is also blessing you with other men who will be fatherly role models for you. You are dearly loved!

Christine, your best friend, Jesus, will help you as you miss your friend. He will hold you close. He knows what it's like when a friend dies. (Check out John 11:17–37.) He will also tell you all about how his resurrection changes the way we look at death, with eyes of hope and life.

Brittany, the love of grandparents is very special. As much as your grandparents loved you, Jesus loves you more. His promise is to help you through this tough time, giving you peace.

Jordan, third base coaches help players run toward home. Jesus promises the same thing. He's going to help you as you run toward your home in heaven.

WHAT'S THE SADDEST THING THAT HAS EVER HAPPENED TO YOU? (TWO OF THREE)

hree girls shared with me something sad in their lives. They are all sad because of some kind of separation. One girl told me the saddest thing was when her parents got divorced. Jackie shared with me how sad she was when she moved away from one of her best friends. And a sad time for Louisa was when she found out her sister was going to high school almost half way around the world.

Being apart from someone you love is very difficult, whether that someone is a parent, a family member, or a friend. We miss them. Our hearts are sad. Things aren't the same.

God knew how hard being away from someone could be. The Holy Spirit led Paul to encourage the people in Rome and all of us through some special words in Romans 8:31–39. He writes, "Who shall separate us from the love of Christ? . . . I am convinced that neither death nor life, neither angels nor demons, neither the present nor the future, nor any powers, neither height nor depth, nor anything else in all creation will be able to separate us from the love of God that is in Christ Jesus our Lord."

While you're missing people in your life, remember those encouraging words!

WHAT'S THE SADDEST THING THAT HAS EVER HAPPENED TO YOU? (THREE OF THREE)

Sara actually had some good news in her answer to this sad question! She said, "I haven't really had anything that sad happen to me." That is great news, Sara! I'm so happy for you! D.J. is doing the chicken dance, and I'm throwing confetti all over the lab! We love to celebrate good news!

Even though we're celebrating with Sara, we also have to face the facts. Here they are:

- We live in a sinful world.

- With sin comes bad and sad things.

- Some day we'll all have to deal with some sad things.

- Because of #3, we need to know God's promises so we'll have extra strength for the sad times.

- God is bigger than any problem we will ever face!

Yikes! I hope those first few facts didn't ruin the party! Thankfully, the last two give us reason to celebrate! Psalm 119:11 talks about hiding God's Word in our hearts. We need to hold on to God's promises so he can use them to comfort us. Celebrate! God's good news can roll over any bad news!

WHAT IS THE BOOK OF ACTS ABOUT?

(A) It's about miracles. (Zachary)

(B) Jesus' actions. (Steven)

(C) Stuff! (Becca)

(D) How you act. (Amanda)

(E) The Acts of the Apostles. (Quincy)

(F) All of the above.

Let's go through each of the answers:

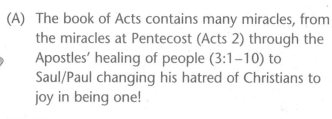

(A) The book of Acts contains many miracles, from the miracles at Pentecost (Acts 2) through the Apostles' healing of people (3:1–10) to Saul/Paul changing his hatred of Christians to joy in being one!

(B) The book begins with the story of Jesus' ascension (going up) into heaven.

(C) How can I argue with Becca's answer? Yes, there's a lot of "stuff" in the book!

(D) This is a clever answer that makes sense! Every book in the Bible gives us examples of how to act. One example in Acts 17:11 tells about a group of people who lived in Berea. It says they received the message with great eagerness and examined the Scriptures every day!

(E) Actually, the official title of this book is "The Acts of the Apostles!" It is filled with stories—stuff—about the apostles' ministry after Jesus returned to heaven.

(F) I'd say "E" is the right answer. Acts is a little bit of all these things! Enjoy reading it!

WHAT iS SOMETHiNG WONDERFUL ABOUT YOUR GRANDPARENTS?

Mike answered that question by saying, "I can do something that isn't that big a deal and they think it's really something." Julie said, "They smile a lot."

Grandparents can be wonderful gifts from heaven, especially if they teach you about Jesus. A wise king named Solomon once wrote: "Grandchildren are like a crown to older people" (Proverbs 17:6 NIrV). You are a blessing to your grandparents! Let them be a blessing to you!

As you think of ways you can bless your grandparents this week, check out these answers I found from kids someone interviewed about grandmothers:

- A grandmother is a lady who has no little children of her own. She likes other people's kids.

- A grandfather is a man grandmother.

- When they take us for walks, they slow down going past things like pretty leaves and caterpillars.

- They can take their teeth and gums out.

- They know we should have snack time before bedtime, and they say prayers with us every time and kiss us even when we've acted badly.

LOL!
(LAUGHING OUT LOUD)

A little boy's prayer: "Dear God, please take care of my daddy and my mommy and my sister and my brother and my doggy and me. Oh, please take care of yourself, God. If anything happens to you, we're gonna be in a big mess."

Our world would be in a HUGE mess without God! But many people say the world is already in a big mess. Does that mean something has happened to God? No, it means something has happened to people. Too many have decided to leave God out of their lives. That's no good! God is the one who comes into our lives and cleans them up. He forgives all who confess their sin. He protects those who trust in him. He shows love to those who love him. He gives wisdom to those who seek it.

Have you ever waited until you're in the middle of making a big mess to remember to call on God? Oops! We are to call on him before, during, and after doing things! God once told his people, "You have turned your backs to me. You refuse to look

at me. But when you are in trouble, you say, 'Come and save us!'" (Jeremiah 2:27 NIrV)

Come now, Lord! Teach us! Help us! Save us! We love you!

WHAT KINDS OF THINGS DID JESUS DO WHEN HE WAS YOUR AGE?

(A) He did carpenter stuff with his dad. (Kristina)

(B) He probably hanged out with his friends. (Sarah)

(C) Studied the Bible and worshiped God. (Emily)

(D) Probably just had a fun life. (Christopher)

(E) All of the above (D.J.)

Those of you who picked D.J.'s answer hit the nail on the head! Congratulations! When Jesus was your age, he did the same things most other pre-teens did, although he did them without sinning!

Only one story in the Bible tells about Jesus when he was your age. Do any of you remember it? Here are some hints: twelve years old . . . the temple . . . talking with and listening to the teachers . . . parents couldn't find him . . . Jesus says, "Didn't you know I had to be in my Father's house?" (Check out Luke 2:41–52.)

Jesus set a good example for us in worshiping his heavenly Father and studying his Word (that's not just for adults, you know!). He did other kid things like spending time with friends and helping his stepfather, Joseph, with his carpentry work. Isn't it great to know Jesus understands perfectly what it's like to be your age?

PRAYER PONDER POINT

Who do you want to pray about more, but often forget?

Kevin knows how important it is to pray for missionaries, but he often forgets to do it. Maybe we all do. Writing down special prayer ideas for missionaries will help us remember them when we pray. List below some things you'd want people to pray for you, if you were a missionary. Can you get the names of some missionaries from your pastor so you can pray for them—or write them? What's on your missionary prayer list?

_____

_____

_____

_____

_____

_____

_____

BiBLE VERSE
FiLL-iN-THE-_____!

"Love is _____, love is _____."

Who's the expert on love around here?
What are the correct answers?

    (A) good—great (Jessie)

    (B) caring—happy (Gary)

    (C) hopeful—kind (Braeden)

    (D) patient—kind (Brooklyn)

According to 1 Corinthians 13 (the "love" chapter), love is patient, love is kind (answer "D"). According to some kids I read about in an email, love is when a girl puts on perfume and a boy puts on shaving cologne, and they go out and smell each other! Another one said that love is when you tell a guy that you like his shirt, and then he wears it everyday.

Families have a special love within them. A girl said, "I know my older sister loves me because she gives me all her old clothes, and then she has to go out and buy new ones!"

One sweetie said, "When my grandmother got arthritis, she couldn't bend over and paint her toenails anymore. So my grandfather does it for her all the time, even though his hands have arthritis too. That's love."

But the bestest act of love (yes, I know bestest isn't a real word) is that Jesus could have made the nails fall off the cross, but he didn't. That's love.

IF JESUS WOULD COME AND TELL YOU ONE THING TODAY, WHAT WOULD HE TELL YOU?

(FIRST OF EIGHT)

You are pretty. That's what one girl hoped Jesus would tell her. You want to know what's really awesome? God sees the beauty in all of us. We see this wrong and that wrong. He sees the beauty of his creation.

There's a book in the Old Testament called Song of Songs. It's a love poem. Some people wonder why it's in the Bible. It's based on words of love between a man and a woman. It shows how much God loves us, his bride, the Church. He wants us to know every part of his beauty as he sees ours. One verse simply says, "You are so beautiful, my love! So beautiful!" Song of Songs 1:15 (NIrV)

I bet you're glad I shared that *beautiful* verse instead of this one from Proverbs 11:22: "A beautiful woman who has no sense is like a gold ring in a pig's nose" (NIrV).

Beautiful, simply beautiful! That's what you are in the eyes of Jesus!

IF JESUS WOULD COME AND TELL YOU ONE THING TODAY, WHAT WOULD HE TELL YOU?
(SECOND OF EIGHT)

Samantha, as well as many others, would like Jesus to tell them, "I love you." Hey Samantha—and all the others who answered with this request—HE DOES!!! "How did God show his love for us? He sent his one and only Son into the world. He sent him so we could receive life through him" (1 John 4:9 NIrV). Not only does he shout his message of love for us across the universe, he shows us his love by sending Jesus to die for us. Because he did, we receive life.

In heaven we will hear Jesus tell us of his love. For now, we live in his love, knowing what he did for us. If you are reading this with others, have them close their eyes while you read the rest of this page. If you're by yourself, look at the rest of the page, close your eyes and picture Jesus in front of you saying these words . . .
Close your eyes . . . Listen.

I love you. I love you, my child. I love you. I love you with all my heart.

I love you. I love you, my child. I love you. I love you with all my heart.

I love you. I love you, my child. I love you. I love you with all my heart.

I love you. I love you, my child. I love you. I love you with all my heart.

I love you. I love you, my child. I love you. I love you with all my heart.

IF JESUS WOULD COME AND TELL YOU ONE THING TODAY, WHAT WOULD HE TELL YOU?
(THIRD OF EIGHT)

Quincy thinks if she ran into Jesus today, her Savior would say to her, "Quincy, go and make disciples!" When you gotta go, you gotta go, right?

That sounds like something God told Jonah. "Hey Jonah, go to Ninevah and make disciples!" (The exact words are in Jonah 1:1–3) The Lord pointed one way, but Jonah went the opposite way!

Sometimes we wonder if it's really that important to show and tell Jesus to other people. But Quincy knows it's very, very, very, very important to Jesus. That's why she knows Jesus wants to make sure we hear his call to go and make disciples. God will set up times when we can show Jesus' love to others. He will give us the words to say. Jesus wants to give heaven to all people, but he uses us to get the news to them about his life, forgiveness, and love.

When you gotta go, you gotta go, right? Go!— because you want to, you know it's important, and because you know what a blessing it is to be his disciple!

If Jesus Would Come and Tell You One Thing Today, What Would He Tell You?
(Fourth of Eight)

Before we get to Katherine's answer, let me ask you. If you were offered a free trip to anywhere, where would you want to go? Would it be someplace you've been before? How did you hear about it? What makes you look forward to going there? How would you get there? Do you know anyone who is there? How much time would you like to spend there?

> God so loved the world that he gave his one and only Son, that whoever believes in him shall not perish but have eternal life.
>
> John 3:16

Now that you did all that thinking, let me tell you how Katherine answered the question about what Jesus would tell her. She thinks he would say, "Katherine, you are going to heaven!" Now there's a trip of a lifetime—more than a lifetime! Forever-time! A life-without-end-time!

As you think about going to heaven someday, answer some of the same questions about your free trip to anywhere:

1. How did you hear about it?

2. What makes you look forward to going there?

3. How would you get there?

4. Do you know anyone who is there?

5. How much time would you like to spend there?

LOL!
(Laughing Out Loud)

Q: Where was Solomon's temple located?

A: On the side of his head!

That cracks me up! (In case you don't know, the softish area between the top of your ear and your eyes is called a temple.) Most of the kids who answered that question said, "Jerusalem" and that really is the correct answer. I was just trying to be funny! Notice I didn't say I was funny, but I was trying to *be* funny!

King David wanted to build a temple to honor and worship God. But the Lord told David his son had been chosen to build the temple instead (2 Samuel 7:4–16). That son was Solomon. The temple would be built in honor of God's name, for worship.

David was, of course, a little disappointed, but he didn't show it. In fact he praised God for letting it be done by his own son. He trusted God's plan. David knew he didn't deserve any of the good things with which God had blessed him. He was just happy to serve him (2 Samuel 7:8–29). That's a great attitude.

Lord, I trust you and your plans. I don't have to get my way. You know and want what is best for me. I will worship your name!

Strange word warning! Strange word warning! Here it comes! Do you know what it means to have *amnesia*? Not too often, but sometimes, people who have accidents that hurt their heads forget things. They might forget where they live, who their family members are, and even what their own names are! That's called amnesia. Usually it goes away. It's hard to imagine waking up and not even knowing your name.

You belong to me.
Isaiah 43:1 niRv

Are you wondering why I told you about amnesia? Hmmm. I forgot. No, I'm just joking. I told you about it because of the way Jason answered our question. He responded, "Jason, you are mine always!"

I have loved you with an everlasting love.
JeRemiah 31:30

Those are great words. "You are mine always!" Cool beans! You don't ever have to wonder if you'll forget who you are—you are a child of God. You belong to God—always! Don't ever forget that! And by the way, it's impossible for God to get amnesia, so he'll never forget you or the fact that you belong to him! Amnesia, spamnesia! You are his . . . always!

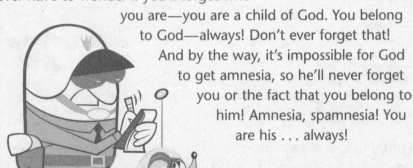

IF JESUS WOULD COME AND TELL YOU ONE THING TODAY, WHAT WOULD HE TELL YOU?
(SIXTH OF EIGHT)

Here are Kelly and Riley's answers:

- Your sins are forgiven. (Kelly)
- Forgive others as you are forgiven. (Riley)

God's forgiveness is amazing, isn't it? Jesus died on the cross to forgive our sins of the past, our present sins, and even our future sins! Amazing! And then he tells us to confess our sins, repent (be truly sorry for them) and be forgiven them. He will forgive them, and the bonus is that he will forget.

And then it makes sense that he would also tell us to forgive others, as we have been forgiven (Luke 6:27). We wouldn't make fun of God by saying, "Please forgive me, Lord, but I'm not going to forgive someone else," would we? So how do we forgive as we have been forgiven?

If we want to get rid of a piece of trash, we throw it in a garbage can. But, it's still there. It's just in another place. It might be possible to burn it, but the ashes are still there. What about hiring a magician to make it disappear? That would just be a trick.

Forgiveness isn't a trick. When Jesus forgives, the garbage (sin) is totally gone. When others ask us to forgive them, we need to let go of the problem between us—give it to Jesus, the Master forgiver! Let those who have sinned against us feel free and forgiven. That's the gift we have in Jesus! Keep giving the gift of forgiveness!

IF JESUS WOULD COME AND TELL YOU ONE THING TODAY, WHAT WOULD HE TELL YOU?
(SEVENTH OF EIGHT)

Seven times in the book of John, Jesus describes himself using the words, "I am."

1. I am the bread of life (John. 6:35–59).

2. I am the light of the world (John 8:12; 9:5; 12:35–36).

3. I am the door (John 10:7–10).

4. I am the good shepherd (John 10:11–18).

5. I am the resurrection and the life (John 11:25).

6. I am the way, the truth and the life (John 14:6).

7. I am the true vine (John 15:1–11).

When I asked Tyler what Jesus would tell him today, he said: I am your Lord and Savior, Tyler.

Jesus is all that and so much more. But it's personal. He's *your* Lord and Savior.

Say those words with your name in the blank:

I am your Lord and Savior, _____.

Say it again.

I am your Lord and Savior, _____.

IF JESUS WOULD COME AND TELL YOU ONE THING TODAY, WHAT WOULD HE TELL YOU?
(EIGHTH OF EIGHT)

- Simon says, "Put your finger in your belly button."

- Did you do it? Simon said to!

- Simon says, "Stick your tongue out and say, 'Jesus is my Rock!'"

- Did you do it? Simon said to!

- Jesus says, "Follow me!"

- Did you do it? It wasn't Simon, but it was Jesus who said to! You can always win if you follow Jesus!

When Caitlyn was asked what she thought Jesus would tell her, she said, "Follow me." Just as Jesus called his disciples, like Peter and Andrew (Matthew 4:18–20), Jesus calls us to do the same! He wants us to give him our lives—to live for him, as he lives for us!

Of course, listening to and following Jesus isn't a game. It's something he's serious about and we should be serious about it too. That doesn't mean we have to wear a serious face all the time! Just take it seriously! It's a joy, not a job, to follow Jesus!

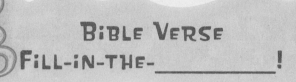

BIBLE VERSE
FILL-IN-THE-_____!

"Then I heard the voice of the Lord. He said, 'Who will I send? Who will go for us?' I said, '_____.'"

The Lord asked something of the prophet Isaiah (Isaiah 6:8). He said, "Who will I send? Who will go for us?" How did Isaiah respond? This is how three kids filled in the blank:

1. Isaiah said: "I will!"

2. Isaiah said: "Jesus will go for us." (In one way, Jesus did go for us. He went to the cross and died for us.)

3. Isaiah said: "Send me. Send me." (Hannah had it right.)

The Lord wants to send us out into our schools, neighborhoods, camps, friend's houses, and the world to share his gifts of grace (undeserved love)!

WHAT IS A PHARISEE?

Let's take a closer look at some answers by putting them under the Dr. Devo microscope. Here's one: "A Pharisee is the name of a sea for tooth fairies—*fairy-sea!*" D.J. made that up!

Let's move on to Kayla. She said a Pharisee is "a man that made sure everyone followed God's law." Pharisees were Jewish religious leaders who were very strict about making sure traditions and God's laws were followed.

Katie said a Pharisee was: "A mean person that took the law too seriously." They were very strict about the laws. Sometimes we talk about them in a mean way because they tried to trick Jesus.

Gina said, "A Pharisee thinks he's God's favorite. He think's he's perfect." Some Pharisees looked down on other people.

That's a quick look at Pharisees. And that's a lot of negative stuff. But if we're honest with ourselves, we often act like Pharisees. We think we're God's favorite—over other people. We often judge others, even though Jesus said, "Do not judge, or you too will be judged" (Matthew 7:1). We need to ask for God's forgiveness, receive it and walk humbly with our God.

LOL!
(Laughing Out Loud)

Sunday school teacher: Manuel, please recite the Ten Commandments for the class.

Manuel: Do they have to be in order?

Teacher: No. They can be in any order.

Manuel: Okay. 2, 7, 9, 1, 3, 10, 5, 6, 8, 4

I don't think that's what the teacher meant! When God gave his commandments to his people, do you think he really meant for them to be obeyed, or did he just offer them as suggestions? I think we all know God always means what he says.

But sometimes we forget that he gave us his commandments because he loves us and knows what's best for us. They are a gift of love. He knows that doing certain things can cause problems in our lives, and he would like to help us avoid those problems. I'm glad God loves us so much that he gave us his commandments to lead us and sent us a Savior for those times when we fail to do what we ought.

You may want to re-read God's Ten Commandments. They are in Exodus 20:1–17.

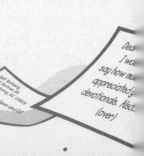

IF YOU COULD ASK THE DISCIPLE PETER ANY QUESTION, WHAT WOULD YOU ASK HIM?

Most of the great kids I interviewed said they would ask him why he denied Jesus three times. But I also received these cool answers:

Cody wants to know why Peter always had something to say about everything. Part of Peter's personality was that he wasn't afraid to speak up. Sometimes that got him into trouble.

Kirsten would ask, "Was Judas a nice guy? Or did he seem like the type of guy who would betray Jesus?" Interesting, Kirsten! Do you think Peter was shocked when Judas betrayed Jesus?

And then Abby had a good question. And I quote, "Dude, how did it feel when you walked on the water?" Peter would probably look at Abby funny and say, "Dude?" Peter really had a lot of amazing experiences with Jesus!

But most importantly, Peter loved Jesus and followed him. Jesus once asked Peter a question three times. It was, "Do you love me?" Peter said, "Lord, you know I love you." Then Jesus told him, "Feed my lambs; take care of my sheep" (John 21:19). In other words, "Take care of my people." That's what following Jesus is all about—loving our Savior and his people!

PRAYER
PONDER POINT

Who do you pray for the most, and why?

John said he prayed for poor people the most because many of us have everything we want and they barely have anything. You have a wonderful heart, John. Part of Jesus' ministry was to bring good news to the poor (Luke 4:18). That's part of our ministry too!

This Prayer Ponder Point has two parts. List some prayer requests for the poor. Then, write down some ways you may be able to help the poor. Pray and serve with confidence and joy!

PRAYERS FOR THE POOR:

_____

_____

_____

_____

_____

_____

245

WAYS I COULD
HELP THE POOR:

_____

_____

_____

_____

_____

_____

_____

OH BROTHER . . . AGAIN

What would it be like to have Jesus as a brother?

Here's how Dana answered that question: "It would be really, really, really cool. Plus every time I sin (and don't know it) he could tell me. That way I can repent."

What a cool thought, Dana! I especially like the thought of repenting for the sins you don't even know about. When you repent of your sins, do you also ask Jesus to forgive those sins you don't even know about? I'm sure we all have a ton of those!

God's people are called to say to God, "Forgive all our sins and receive us graciously" (Hosea 14:2). It doesn't say, "Forgive the sins we know about." No, forgive them all—even those we don't know about.

And I hope you're not surprised with Jesus' answer when you pray that: "I forgive you *all* your sins— even those you don't know about.

LOL!
(Laughing Out Loud)

Q: What excuse did Adam give his children to explain why they got kicked out of the Garden of Eden?

A: He said, "Your mother ate us out of house and home."

Do you love to eat? I do! I don't always eat the best foods though. That's bad for me. Here's one of my favorite recipes.

Potato Chip Salad

Empty three different flavors of potato chips into one very large bowl. Mix and serve.

By the way, feel free to put my "Potato Chip Salad" in your family recipe book! As you do that, remember that all who have food to eat—humans, plants, and animals—can praise and give thanks to God! Psalm 104:27 reminds us, "These all look to you to give them their food at the proper time."

Chew on that good news for a while, and then give thanks to God for it!

WHAT IS A PSALM?

Did anyone give me the correct answer? Here's what I collected:

- A song
- A prayer
- A Bible book
- A palm tree

They are songs! They are prayers! Put them all together, and it's a book in the Bible—150 psalms in one book! But no, a psalm is not a palm tree!

Some psalms are happy. Some are sad. Different people wrote the psalms—from David to court musicians. And Moses even wrote one (Psalm 90)! Some are long. Others are short. Here's one of the short ones you can use as a prayer of praise today. It's Psalm 100.

Shout for joy to the Lord,
  all the earth.
Worship the Lord with gladness;
Come before him with joyful songs.
Know that the Lord is God.
It is he who made us, and we are his;
We are his people, the sheep of his
  pasture.
Enter his gates with thanksgiving
  and his courts with praise;
Give thanks to him and praise his name.
  for the Lord is good
  and his love endures forever;
His faithfulness continues through
  all generations.

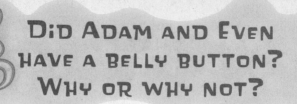

DID ADAM AND EVEN HAVE A BELLY BUTTON? WHY OR WHY NOT?

The vote on this question was very close! If I remember correctly, it was something like 50 percent had answers like Casey: "No, because they weren't born" and the other 50 percent answered it like Aaron: "Yes, all humans have one!" That's a pretty close vote!

I couldn't find the answer in the Bible, so I wrote to the top navel officer to find the answer, but he didn't know either. Then I called the president of the Navel Orange Growers Association, but she hung up on me! I guess what I'm trying to tell you—as D.J. cleans the lint out of his belly button—is that I don't know the answer!

But here's what I do know. Adam and Eve were created by God. They didn't just show up with a *poof*. They didn't evolve from some animal. The Bible clearly says that he created both and Adam and Eve. Read Genesis 2:4–25 to get the whole scoop. I just wish that when God made sure the story of creation was in the Bible, he had told us whether or not the first people had belly buttons! Oh well, it's not a big a deal, is it? Let's just praise him for the miracle of creation!

WHAT MAKES YOU HAPPiEST?

Mandi answered that question by saying, "When my dog licks my face!" And I love the way Derek worded his happiness answer. He said, "My cat makes me feel delighted! Pets are a fun gift from God. They can bring people a lot of happiness!"

If you're reading this with someone else, have them think about what makes them happiest, but tell them not to say it yet. Then give yourself three chances to see if you can guess what their answers would be. That could be a fun way to learn about others! Then let them try and guess what makes you happiest.

Meghan had an awesome answer. She said she is happiest knowing that when she dies she will be saved. Awesome! No fear of death. Jesus defeated it on the cross! Meghan knows heaven is hers as a gift from Jesus! That should make us all very happy, because it is our gift too!

When Paul wrote about death and resurrection, he quoted the prophet Isaiah saying, "Death has been swallowed up in victory" (1 Corinthians 15:54).

Thanks, Jesus, for the gift of happiness. Thanks especially for the gift of heaven, where we will be perfectly happy!

WHAT DO YOU THINK THE COLOR OF JESUS' SKIN MIGHT BE?

- Sort of dark because people from that area are sort of tan. (Adoria)

- White, because he is white in movies and pictures. (Amber)

- Black, because most people think he was white. (Katie)

Depending on where you live or travel, you may have seen many pictures of Jesus—all looking very different. Here are a few secrets you may already know:

1. Being born as a Jew in Bethlehem, he would have looked like someone from that region— with darker skin—like those from Israel today.

2. He wouldn't have looked like he was from the United States, the way so many movies and pictures show him.

3. Skin color doesn't matter to Jesus, and it shouldn't matter to us either.

God asks us to love all people, and look at them as his children. Don't judge them by their skin color, weight, height, hairstyle, or anything else. There is no difference!

> There is no difference between Jew and Gentile—the same Lord is Lord of all and richly blesses all who call on him.
>
> ROMANS 10:12

BiBLE VERSE
FiLL-iN-THE-_____!

Jesus said, "I am the Vine; you are the _____.

Is your mind blank for this fill-in-the-blank, or do you know the answer?

(A) Branches (Sally and many others)

(B) Fruit (Allyson and Cody)

(C) Grapes (Andrea and James)

(D) Leaf (Dan)

(E) Roots (Carly)

The answer is in John 15:5. (If you don't have time to look it up, check out Sally's answer!)

That verse reminds me that I need to water my garden. So I'm going to let you figure out your own devotion for this one. Think about the following questions while I water the plants.

1. How do branches live? How do they get food to grow?

2. Can a branch live if it's cut off from the vine?

3. If branches grow out of the vine, what grows out of the branches?

4. Why would Jesus say he is the Vine and we are the branches?

IF YOU COULD ASK THE APOSTLE PAUL ANY QUESTION, WHAT WOULD YOU ASK HIM? (FIRST OF FOUR)

Amanda was interested in asking him, "Why did you persecute people?"

Before Paul became a great missionary for Jesus Christ, he used to persecute (hurt and kill) Christians! Back then he was known by the name of Saul. When his heart was changed—thanks to God—he received a name change and a change of plans. He would spend his life living for Jesus and spreading the news about him.

So why did he want to get rid of Christians at first? Paul didn't know Jesus was the Savior—*his* Savior. He didn't realize Jesus was the Messiah, mentioned in the Old Testament. More and more people were following Jesus—becoming Christians. He and other leaders wanted to get rid of Christians so they wouldn't take over. The story of Paul's change of heart is really cool. It's in Acts 9:1–19 if you would like to read it.

Paul was so amazed that God would love him and use him after what he had done. He once wrote this, "Christ Jesus came into the world to save sinners. And I am the worst sinner of all. But for that very reason, God showed me mercy . . . I was an example for those who would come to believe in him." (1 Timothy 1:15 NIrV).

IF YOU COULD ASK THE APOSTLE PAUL ANY QUESTION, WHAT WOULD YOU ASK HIM? (SECOND OF FOUR)

Allyson would like to ask this of Paul, "How did you get to be such a good writer?" Paul would give the Holy Spirit all the credit for his writing. His writings were really letters to different churches he once served or churches he had heard about. Some were to support and encourage individuals. He was a letter writer! A very powerful one! Why? The Holy Spirit gave him the words, and he had a great love for Jesus and his message.

With that thought in our minds, let's go to Jackie's question for Paul: "How did it feel to reach so many people with a special message?" I don't want to put words in Paul's mouth, but I'm pretty sure he would tell you, Jackie, that he was humbled by it and honored to do it. He knew it was the message that Jesus used to save him, and he wanted others to be saved. He had a passion for it!

When Paul wrote the second letter to the young pastor Timothy, he began with these words, "I, Paul, am writing this letter. I am an apostle of Christ Jesus, just as God planned. He sent me to tell about the promise of life that is found in Christ Jesus" (2 Timothy 1:1 NIrV). Those words tell a lot about how he loved Jesus and loved to share his message of salvation!

If you Could ask the apostle Paul any question, what would you ask Him? (Third of four)

If Kyle could interview the apostle Paul, he would ask, "What was it like to be arrested so many times?" And Cody would want to add, "Were you scared when you were in prison?"

Paul was arrested a lot. He shared the message of Jesus, and many people didn't like that. Before he became a follower of Jesus, he tried to stop Christians from sharing the news of the Savior. Now others were trying to stop him! And the devil *certainly* wanted to stop the spread of the saving news of Jesus!

I'm sure there were times when Paul was very discouraged as people tried to stop him. But I also know he trusted in God to use even those times when he was in prison for good. In fact, he wrote these words in Romans 8:28 (NIrV), "We know that in all things God works for the good of those who love him."

When you go through bad times, remember those words of encouragement from Paul. God is working for your good—even when others mean it for bad!

If you could ask the apostle Paul any question, what would you ask him? (Fourth of four)

If Kristen could, she'd ask Paul, "What was your favorite place you've traveled?

Paul got to travel to many places. He was a traveling missionary. The Bible tells us of three different missionary trips he took, going from city to city. He traveled to Rome, Spain, and cities like Jerusalem, Ephesus, Philippi, and many others!

Again, I don't know how Paul would answer that question, but I wouldn't be surprised if he told us his favorite place was wherever he went to spread the good news of Jesus! We might travel to those places for vacation, but Paul was on a mission! He didn't take shopping trips to Rome to get the latest Italian sandals. He didn't take rolls of pictures of different landmarks when he traveled by boat. His mission was to share Jesus with all he met. He loved Jesus. He loved God's people. And he had such a great love for people who didn't believe in Jesus that he traveled to get the word out!

Here's an example of the way he thought about his travels. It's from Romans 1:14–15 (NIrV), "I have a duty both to Greeks and to non-Greeks. I have a duty both to wise people and to foolish people. So I really want to preach the good news also to you who live in Rome."

Send me, Lord, on a mission for you!

LOL!
(Laughing Out Loud)

Dylan said that one of his favorite jokes is:

> Q: What doesn't move but runs around the house?
>
> A: A fence.

D.J. made up this one, with a similar answer (you don't have to laugh):

> Q: What doesn't move much but just runs around the house of a really bad football team?
>
> A: "De fence!"

In Psalm 27:4, David has one request of God. He wants to spend all his time in God's house—God's presence. There will probably be days when he wants to run around and praise God. At other times, he probably won't move. He'll just gaze on the beauty of God's presence, promises, and love.

That's a great prayer for all of us. Here are the words. I hope you'll pray:

> One thing I ask of the Lord, this is what I seek: that I may dwell in the house of the Lord all the days of my life, to gaze upon the beauty of the Lord and to seek him in his temple.
>
>
> PSALM 27:4

GUILT QUESTION #1: WHAT IS SOMETHING THAT MAKES YOU FEEL REALLY GUILTY?

Here are some of the responses I got for this question:

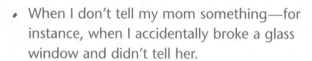

- When I hurt other people's feelings.

- When I start something and don't finish it.

- When I fight with my brother or sister.

- When I don't tell my mom something—for instance, when I accidentally broke a glass window and didn't tell her.

- When I make someone cry.

- When I lie.

Sometimes we feel guilty even when we haven't done anything wrong. But usually, it is a feeling that comes with sin. It's kind of an alarm in our minds that tells us when we've messed up. How should we react to it? We should confess our sin to God. We should ask others to forgive us if we have hurt them in some way. And then we should allow God to forgive our sin and also our guilt.

David wrote this about guilt and God's forgiveness: "Then I admitted my sin to you. I didn't cover up the wrong I had done . . . And you forgave the guilt of my sin" (Psalm 32:4 NIrV).

Guilt question #2:
Who are some people who cause you to feel guilty?

This question got some interesting answers, like:

- Mom
- Dad
- Grandparents
- Teachers
- I do
- The devil

Imagine your parents telling you to clean out the cage for your pet worm, hamster, or lion but you don't do it. Two days later your parents ask you about it. You feel guilty. Your parents didn't cause you to feel guilty—disobeying your parents made you feel that way! Ugh!

Or maybe your book report on *Dr. Devo's New-Fangled, Lickety-Split Devotions* is due on Friday, but on the following Tuesday, you still don't have it finished. Your teacher talks to you about it, and you feel guilty. It's not your teacher's fault—it's your fault.

Many times it's not people who make us feel guilty, but they are the ones who point out that we've done something wrong. Maybe you have felt like David, who wrote, "My guilt has become too much for me. It is a load too heavy to carry" (Psalm 38:4 NIrV).

We can rejoice that our sin and its guilt wasn't too heavy for Jesus to carry to the cross so we could have forgiveness! Thank you, forgiving Savior!

GUILT QUESTION #3: HOW DO YOU TRY TO GET OVER FEELING GUILTY ABOUT SOMETHING?

(A) Pray.

(B) Do something else.

(C) Sleep.

(D) Watch TV.

(E) Ask for forgiveness.

Those are a few of the answers kids gave me. Do you try any of them to get over guilty feelings? What works? What doesn't work?

People try many things to stop feeling guilty. Taking a nap will stop the guilt for a while. You might even wake up feeling a little better. Watching TV takes your mind off it, but you still have to deal with it sooner or later! It doesn't go away!

> Let us come near to God with an honest and true heart. Let us come near with a faith that is sure and strong ... Our minds have been cleansed from a sense of guilt.
>
> HEBREWS 10:22 nirv

Only one thing will take it away. Pray or ask for forgiveness! Accept the forgiveness of Jesus! Trust in his promise to totally get rid of your sin. Know that if God forgives you, you should also forgive yourself.

GUILT QUESTION #4: WHAT DOES IT FEEL LIKE TO BE GUILTY?

One boy's answer tells the whole story about how guilt feels. He told me "It's a horrible feeling." Horrible is very bad.

You've probably seen TV shows where people are arrested for their crimes. They have to go to court, and a judge or jury decides if they are guilty of the crimes or not. One lawyer will try to show the judge a person's guilt. Another one will try to prove his or her innocence.

After thinking about that, listen to John 16:8. Jesus tells about one of the works of the Holy Spirit. He says, "When [the Holy Spirit] comes, he will convict the world of guilt in regard to sin." In other words, he will prove that the world's people are guilty. He will show us our sin. We're guilty. We should be convicted. But thankfully, God decides what should happen to his followers by looking at the perfect life of Jesus. He announces that we are not guilty because Jesus has died in our place! Can you even imagine? Wow! We go from feeling horrible to feeling thankful, wanting to always live for Jesus who has saved us!

WHO OR WHAT SCARES YOU THE MOST?

I have something to say before looking at some of the answers I received. What I want to say is . . . BOOOOOO!

Okay, now that I got that out of my system, here are some things that scare kids your age:

- Snakes

- Being alone at night

- Rats

- Aliens

- The devil

Something (or someone) scares each of us. That's natural. But God doesn't want us to live in fear. He didn't create us to be weak and scared all the time. When Paul wanted to encourage a young pastor named Timothy, one of the things he said to him was, "God didn't give us a spirit that makes us weak and fearful. He gave us a spirit that gives us power and love" (2 Timothy 1:7 NIrV).

Every once in a while you might go "BOO-HOO" when someone yells, "BOOOO!" But now you can yell "YAHOO" cause Jesus loves YOU!

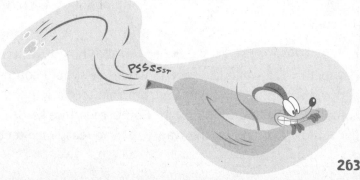

PSSSSsт

BIBLE VERSE
FILL-IN-THE-_____!

"The king said to the woman, 'Your teeth are as clean as a
_____.'"

Yes, this really is in the Bible! The king is trying to tell the woman he loves how beautiful she is. Picture him holding her in his arms and looking into her eyes. The candles are burning, and he says to her, "Sweetheart, your teeth are as clean as a clean floor." That's what Tammy thought the answer was!

Take two! LaVern will provide the answer this time. The candles are glowing. He looks into her eyes and says, "Honey, your teeth are as clean as a mom!"

And if D.J. were the king, he'd say, "Hey sweets, your teeth are as clean as my plate after supper!" He's so romantic! But the answer is "Your teeth are as clean as a flock of sheep" (Song of Songs 4:2 NIrV). Really!

We may not think that's the best compliment, but he meant it as one. Her teeth were white like sheep's wool. We should compliment people more, shouldn't we? We complain too much and don't compliment each other enough! Compliment! Be kind! Encourage! Oh, and by the way, you have really nice teeth!

LOL!
(LAUGHING OUT LOUD)

Amanda has a favorite knock-knock joke. It goes like this:

> Knock-knock.
>
> Who's there?
>
> Dishes.
>
> Dishes who?
>
> Dishes your friend. Open the door!

I'll have to remember that dish joke, Amanda, and serve it up to some of my friends! So tell me who your best, best, best friend is in the universe? It's Jesus! He calls us, and all of his disciples, "friends" (John 15:14). Plus, he comes to visit us! He loves spending time with us. And guess what! He stands at the door of our hearts and knocks! He says, "Dish is your friend! I'm ready to serve you!" Well, he doesn't say that exactly. Here's what he says, according to Revelation 3:20, "Here I am! I stand at the door and knock. If anyone hears my voice and opens the door, I will come in and eat with him, and he with me."

Knock, knock! Are you going to open the door?

WHAT iS AN EPiSTLE?

At first I didn't get Ben's answer, but then it made me laugh! Ben said an epistle was a gun! (A pistol!) There were more creative answers. Andrea said an epistle is a "non-apostle." And James thought it might be a place where apostles lived.

But Michelle and others had the right answer. An epistle is a letter. The New Testament is filled with epistles or letters written by Paul and others to churches, groups of believers, or individual people. The New Testament epistles are:

- Romans
- 1 & 2 Corinthians
- Galatians
- Ephesians
- Philippians
- Colossians
- 1 & 2 Thessalonians
- 1 & 2 Timothy
- Titus
- Philemon
- Hebrews
- James
- 1 & 2 Peter
- 1, 2, & 3 John
- Jude

The first chapters of these letters tell you who wrote them and who they were written to. They were written on scrolls. Check out 1 Timothy 1:1–2 or Galatians 1:1–3. Who wrote these letters? To whom were they written? Before you check, close with this blessing that Paul uses in many of his epistles: "Grace and peace to you from God our Father and the Lord Jesus Christ."

IF JESUS WOULD ASK YOUR PARENTS ONE QUESTION TODAY, WHAT WOULD HE ASK?
(FIRST OF FIVE)

What one question do you think Jesus would ask your parents? One girl thinks he would ask, "Do you think your child is a little angel?" If that was what he asked your parents, how do you think they'd answer (once they stopped laughing, of course)? Don't all parents think their children are little angels?

Let's see what angels are all about:

1. Psalm 148:2 says that angels praise God. Hey, you do that!

2. Angels help protect people, according to Psalm 91:11. Two for two. You can do that also!

3. Angels minister to (serve) Jesus and others (Matthew 4:11). You serve!

4. Matthew 22:30 says that angels don't marry. Well, three out of four isn't bad! I know you're not married now, but someday you might be.

5. Angels don't know when Jesus will return (Matthew 24:26) and neither do you!

6. Angels rejoice when someone repents (Luke 15:10). Hey, you do that too!

7. Heaven's angels are without sin (2 Peter 2:4). Big OOPS! Okay, so you're not a prefect little angel . . . but you are dearly loved, and there's no question about that!

If Jesus would ask your parents one question today, what would he ask? (Second of five)

Three kids ... three parents ... one Savior ... one question for each parent:

1. Do you believe in me?

2. Is there a cross in your house?

3. Do you go to church?

It sounds like some of these kids are interested in something very important. It's the faith of their parents. If you were blessed with parents who love the Lord, thank them—and God! Not every child knows what that is like. Some parents don't believe in Jesus as their Savior even though their children do. Some children have to walk to church because their parents won't take them. Some children don't see any signs of Jesus in their homes (not that Christians have to have crosses in their homes).

Would you do these children a HUGE favor? Please pray for their parents. Pray for the children too. In fact, pray for the faith of each person living in their homes. And then pray for the faith of your own parents. Ask your parents if they have any special prayer requests. And if your parents don't believe in Jesus—but you do— know that others are praying for all of you! God bless you as you grow in his love!

IF JESUS WOULD ASK YOUR PARENTS ONE QUESTION TODAY, WHAT WOULD HE ASK? (THIRD OF FIVE)

1. Has your son been good?

2. Does your daughter try her best to stay true to me?

If Jesus asked your parents questions like those, he would know the answers already, right? He knows all things. He would know the answer better than your parents! Many times Jesus asked people questions he knew the answers to already. Sometimes he did that to make them think about the question.

How do you think you would answer those two questions—about yourself? How would your parents answer them? At times we are good, while many other times we aren't. We try to stay true to Jesus, but often we don't try our hardest.

That's why it's so good to know we live every day in the forgiveness, mercy, and love of Jesus. Otherwise, there wouldn't be any hope! We can also pray for help using the words of David, from Psalm 86:11 (NIrV), "Lord, teach me how you want me to live. Then I will follow your truth. Give me a heart that doesn't want anything more than to worship you."

One girl thinks Jesus would ask her parents, "How much do you love your children?" I hope you know how much your parents love you. They probably love you even more than you know or imagine!

"I love you!" Some families don't even say those three important words to each other. That doesn't mean they don't love each other; they just show their love in other ways. But D.J. and I think we should start a "Say I Love You" campaign. Those are wonderful words to hear and to share—*if* you mean them! Make sure your actions go along with your words!

Try them out on your mom or dad. How about your grandparents? If you have brothers or sisters, those words could change their day. An aunt or uncle? Go ahead! It's not hard. They're only three words, but they have a very important message! Let's see, did we forget anyone? Oh yeah . . .

I love you, LORD!
PSALM 18:1 niRv

IF JESUS WOULD ASK YOUR PARENTS ONE QUESTION TODAY, WHAT WOULD HE ASK? (FIFTH OF FIVE)

One boy thought Jesus would ask his parents, "I suspect you're reading the Bible too, right?" Now this is just a guess, but I wonder if this boy's parents are wanting him to read his Bible! He may be wanting to check to see if they're reading it too!

We may not think too often about what an amazing gift God's Word, the Bible, is. But it contains everything we need to know to be saved, to live our lives, and to find help through our powerful and loving God. It's filled with hope, peace, correction, comfort, stories of God's people, stories of God's direction, teachings, and so much more! Thank you, God, for sharing your Word with us. Help us as we read it to let it direct our lives in the way you want us to go!

Direct my footsteps according to your word.
Psalm 119:133

WHAT'S THE FIRST SENTENCE IN THE BIBLE?

Steven and many others knew the answer was "In the beginning God created the heavens and the earth" (Genesis 1:1). But there were two funny guys who wrote this as their answer to the question, "What is the first sentence in the Bible?" Ready for this? They said, "New International Version of the Holy Bible!" Funny guys! That's the name of the *translation* of the Bible. But they have a point. I guess it's the first thing in their Bibles ... but it's not really a sentence, is it? Ha! So that won't work!

Here's another cool way to say how the Bible starts. You can just take the first four words, "In the beginning ... God! He's what it's all about. He was there in the beginning, yet he had no beginning and he will have no end. He is the creator of every molecule, every leaf of spinach, every nose hair, heart, rock, planet, mountain, blade of grass, man, woman, child, monkey, flea, and where does it end? It's *all* about God. In the beginning ... God ... forever and ever.

Worship the Creator of everything in the skies (heavens) and the earth! He is your God! And he loves loving you!

PRAYER
PONDER POINT

I talked to a young boy in the hospital who has cancer. I asked him, "Who do you pray for the most, and why?" His answer was, "My mom, because she needs it."

Not only is it tough being sick. It's also hard on the family. With this Prayer Ponder Point we're going to focus on families who have children (or other relatives) in the hospital or sick at home. We're going to pray for those family members who take care of them. What kind of special prayers do you think they might need? Do you know anyone who takes care of someone who is sick? Write your prayer thoughts below, and pray for these special people who are gifts from heaven.

_____

_____

_____

_____

_____

_____

What Does it
Mean to "Tithe?"

Mr. Comedian, Ben, said it's when two people win a race. (You know what, I'm not sure he even knows how funny he is!) Callie and Rick said it means to give ten percent of all you have. And D.J. is pointing to my neck. No, I'm not wearing a bow tithe! That's a bow *tie*!

You may not know what ten percent (sometimes we just call it "a tenth") means. It's a math term. For instance, a tenth of a dollar is ten cents. A tenth of ten dollars is one dollar. In the Old Testament, God asked that his people give one tenth of what they earned toward his work. That might have been in money or maybe a farmer's crops.

Even though many of us don't live under that commandment any more, it's a very good guide for us as we give to the Lord. God wanted at least a tenth to help spread his good news. Some people may tithe, but they won't give love to others. That isn't what giving is all about. In Matthew 23:23, Jesus jumps all over the Pharisees. He says, "How terrible for you, teachers of the law and Pharisees! You pretenders! You give God a tenth of your spices ... but you have not practiced the more important things of the law, like fairness, mercy and faithfulness."

The most important thing to remember is that "God loves a cheerful giver" (2 Corinthians 9:7).

WHERE DO YOU THINK THE GREATEST PLACE IN THE WORLD IS LOCATED?

Some kids think these are the greatest places in the world:

(A) Jenna—Mora, Missouri, because it's in the country.

(B) Matthew—Six Flags, because it has all the cool rides.

(C) Audra—Mount Rushmore, because it is cool.

(D) Katherine—Yellowstone Park, because the animals run free.

(E) Nicole—Eden, because it was perfect.

Those are all great places. (Even though I've never heard of Mora, Missouri, I trust Jenna!) Maybe you want to add some more. While you're thinking, what about these great places in God's creation?

- The stable-like place where Jesus was born.

- The hill where Jesus died.

- The tomb where he rose from the dead.

- And don't forget the place where he created faith in you and made you a new creation, because "if anyone is in Christ, he is a new creation; the old has gone, the new has come!" (2 Corinthians 5:17).

275

WHAT'S THE MOST EMBARRASSING THING YOU'VE EVER DONE?

- Called a male teacher "mom!" (Joel)

- Hitting a homer, running around the bases, and then being told that I was out because I threw the bat. (Louisa)

- I wore my dad's under-wear on my head when I was little. (Andrea)

- Running into a glass door when it was closed. (Michelle)

- When I got out of the pool and my shorts almost came down. (No name!)

- I was on the monkey bars and my pants fell down. (I'll keep his name a secret too!)

- And Allyson simply said, "I'm not telling!"

We've all done all sorts of funny, silly, and embarrassing things. And I think that we should just let this devotion be a time of thinking funny things. If you're by yourself, just think funny thoughts! What have you done that is embarrassing?

Just smile and have fun! And remember, "A cheerful heart enjoys a good time that never ends" (Proverbs 15:15 NIrV).

BiBLE VERSE
FiLL-iN-THE-_____!

The Lord said, "Before you were born I knew _____
_____."

Pick your answer! Will it be A, B, C, or D?

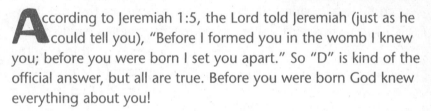

   (A) The color of your hair (Mandy)

   (B) What you looked like (Kyle)

   (C) When you would be born (Cory)

   (D) You (many kids)

   (E) All the above

According to Jeremiah 1:5, the Lord told Jeremiah (just as he could tell you), "Before I formed you in the womb I knew you; before you were born I set you apart." So "D" is kind of the official answer, but all are true. Before you were born God knew everything about you!

- He knew the color of your hair!

- He knew the day you'd be born even though your parents didn't know exactly!

- He knew about that embarrassing thing you would do . . . well, let's just forget that!

- He knew that you'd be reading this devotion right now!

- He knew he'd love you and set you apart to be someone special in his kingdom! He has great plans for you!

LOL!
(LAUGHING OUT LOUD)

Allison wants to share her favorite joke with you:

> Q: What kind of ring did the rabbit give his girlfriend?
>
> A: A 14 carrot gold ring.

Of all the gifts you've received for your birthday, what was your favorite? What about a favorite Christmas present? Who gave you this book? Or did you buy it yourself? Receiving gifts is fun, and so is giving them!

Gifts come in all shapes and sizes. Some people like to wrap their presents in really weird shapes so people can't guess what they are. Others wrap things in the shape of the present itself. That makes it easy to guess if you're getting a fishing pole, a ball, or a flute.

> I pray to the God of our Lord Jesus Christ. God is the glorious Father. I keep asking him to give you the wisdom and understanding that come from the Holy Spirit. I want you to know God better.
>
> EPHESIANS 1:17

God gives us gifts every day. He wraps them in his love and surprises us with his kindness. When Paul wrote the church in Ephesus, he told them about a present he asked God to give them. It's my prayer for you too!

WHAT'S THE WEIRDEST PART OF YOUR BODY?

old on for the answers I got to that question:

- Belly button (because there's a hole there)

- Ears

- My elbow, because it's double jointed

- Feet

- The funny bone

- The face, because it wrinkles up

> How you made me is amazing and wonderful. I praise you for that. What you have done is wonderful. I know that very well.
>
> PSALM 139:14 NIRV

We may think some of our body parts are really weird. But God made every one for a reason—even those parts we call private. If you think about it, the body is a constant miracle. We can stand, run, sit, breathe, move, see, smell, taste, and so much more.

Thank you, Lord, for the miracle of my body!

BIBLE VERSE
FILL-IN-THE-_____!

Jesus said, "He who has an ear, let him _____."

You have some interesting choices here. What do you think?

(A) Have a nose (Jeremy)

(B) Listen (Dave)

(C) Listen to his mother (DJ's mom)

(D) Clean them! (DJ's mom)

Dave (B) is the closest, so we'll give it to him! Many times in the book of Revelation, Jesus said, "He who has an ear, let him hear" (Revelation 13:9). He said this to get people to listen. He wants them to know that what he has to say is important. He has given us ears for hearing, so he wants us to listen up!

Everything Jesus says is important. In the book of Revelation, he talks about the last days and heaven. He wants to make sure people know the way to heaven—through Jesus Christ alone! He wants to change our hearts to make them more like his. Jesus wants people to listen and then also to do what he says.

Look in the mirror. Do you have ears? Then listen! Jesus has important, life-saving, and life-changing things to say to you!

HAVE YOU BEEN TO A FUNERAL OR FUNERAL HOME? WHAT WERE YOUR THOUGHTS ABOUT IT?

- "Yes. One time it was especially sad." (Christopher)

- "Very sad, especially since the person had two young kids and died suddenly." (Joel)

Even though we know we can't ignore death, there are many reasons some parents choose not to take their children to funerals or funeral homes. We do need to remember that death is part of life on earth. As long as we are hanging out on earth, people will die.

Funerals and funeral homes can be very sad. Maybe you're not comfortable with them. Death doesn't make us comfortable. It doesn't seem right. That's because it's wrong. It's not the way God created the world.

When Adam and Eve first lived in Eden, there was no death. Death came into the world along with sin. Adam and Eve had to deal with death in their family when Cain killed Abel. It's interesting that after Abel was killed, Adam and Eve had another son (one of many children they would have). They named him Seth. When Seth grew it says, "At that time men began to call on the name of the Lord" (Genesis 4:26).

The next time you go to a funeral, don't forget to call on the name of the Lord. Ask him to show you ways you can show kindness to the family of the person who died. Give him thanks for his presence and promises. Call on the name of the Lord ... but don't wait until something bad happens! Call out now!

WHAT KINDS OF THINGS DO PASTORS DO BESIDES PREACH?

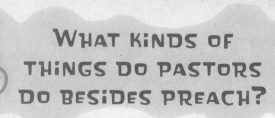

Some people think pastors only work on Sunday! That's not true. I thought I'd check with some kids to get their ideas. Steven said pastors eat chips and play golf. (I'm not going to comment on that!) James said they move around. Some pastors do move where God leads them, in order to better serve his people. Pam said that pastors talk to people about their problems. And that is part of a pastor's calling—helping others and trying, with God's help, to deal with their problems. Lydia gets right to the point: "They sleep, eat, and do everything we do!"

Pastors are ordinary people. But God has called them to teach his people in a special way—as full-time church workers. If you've thought about serving God in this way, you might want to read three books in the Bible that Paul wrote to pastors. They give good advice to pastors. Those books are 1 Timothy, 2 Timothy, and Titus.

Don't forget to pray for your pastor! Together we serve an awesome God!

WHAT DO YOU THINK ADAM AND EVE TALKED ABOUT?

I thought I'd get lots of fun answers to this question, but most kids couldn't think of anything. One girl did say she thought they talked about which new plants were growing! I don't know if they talked about that, but I know Jesus talked about plants in some of his parables. Do you know the parable of the sower? It's in Luke 8:4–8. I hope you have time to read it! When you're finished, look for the meaning of the parable. Jesus explains it a few verses later, in Luke 8:11–15.

Then talk about the following questions:

1. What is a parable?

2. Why do you think Jesus used parables to teach the people?

3. What is something new you learned from the parable?

4. What does the seed stand for?

5. What does the last line in verse 8:15 mean—what kind of crop do God's faithful people produce?

LOL!
(Laughing Out Loud)

Judy e-mailed this joke to the Dr. Devo lab. I thought you might enjoy it!

> Q: Why did the pilgrims have problems with their pants falling down?

> A: Because they wore their belt buckles on their hats!

What's up with that? Pilgrim pictures do show the men wearing hats with belt buckles on them, don't they?
That seems silly!

I've seen stranger things. I've seen people wearing earrings on other parts of their bodies, besides their ears! Ouch! Doesn't that hurt? It's also not the safest thing in the world. Personally, I, Dr. Devo, am not crazy about piercings, tattoos, or belt buckles on hats. For health reasons, I wouldn't suggest them. (A belt buckle on a hat isn't unhealthy, just different.) I think whether things are good ideas or not, often depends on the reason you're doing them. If you're wearing a buckle on your hat or an earring somewhere other than your ear, are you doing it just to get attention, or is there a God-pleasing reason for it? When you get older and think about these things, ask Jesus for his advice.

BIBLE VERSE
FiLL-iN-THE-_____!

"If God is for us, who can _____?"

    (A) Be against us (Christopher)

    (B) Not be happy (Marco)

    (C) Like us (Samantha)

    (D) Beat that (Karl)

Did you guess (or know) the answer? It's from Romans 8:31. If you don't know, let me give you *A* clue! How's that for a clue! But I also like the other thoughts:

If God is for us, who cannot be happy" (or be unhappy)? We will have many sad times in our lives. But the good news that comes with knowing Jesus is that there can always be happiness in our lives, too, through him!

If God is for us, who can like us? There are many places in the Bible that warn us that if we stand up for Jesus, people may not like us. Totally living for Jesus won't make us the most popular people. But God is on our side! So who can be against us?

If God is for us, who can beat that? Great answer, Karl! You're right, nothing can beat the news that God is on our side. He's in our corner. He's fighting for us. He's protecting us. He loves us! Who can beat that?!

WHAT'S THE MOST CONFUSING THING IN THE BIBLE? (FIRST OF TWO)

These answers came to our lab from some of you confused kids!

- The chariot of fire
- The devil
- What happened to Samson
- The names of people

And Kirsten wrapped it all up in a way that wasn't confusing at all! She said what confuses her are "the words on the pages!"

Maybe these ideas will help as you read and study God's Word:

1. Pray that the Holy Spirit will help you understand the Word better.

2. When you come to something you don't understand, write it down so you can either ask someone later, look it up in a book about the Bible, or just keep track of it as something you want to learn more about.

3. When you're confused, ask someone for help. Those around you may not know the answer, but you can all grow and learn together.

4. Keep a journal as you study the Bible. Write down what you learned, what questions you have, and what things you want to pray about.

God will bless you and your study of his life-saving Word! "Your word is truth" (John 17:17).

WHAT'S THE MOST CONFUSING THING IN THE BIBLE? (SECOND OF TWO)

Most pre-teens said the book of Revelation was the most confusing thing in the Bible. A few said the parables confused them. Since so many admitted Revelation confused them, I decided to ask one girl what the book of Revelation is about. She responded, "I don' t know—YET!" I like her honesty and the way she is looking forward to learning more about God's Word! She doesn't know—YET!

Revelation is the most difficult book to understand because the writing is so different. Jesus gave John a peek at heaven and gave a "revelation" to him. Heaven is so beyond our minds' understanding! That makes it confusing. Different people explain it in different ways. It is best to study Revelation with your pastor, who can really help you understand it. Revelation is an important book with its teachings about Christ's return and heaven. It is just difficult.

I'll give you a peek into the book by writing out the first verses—the ones that tell what it's about. Revelation 1:1–3 (NIrV) reads, "This is the revelation that God gave to Jesus. Christ Jesus shows those who serve God what will happen soon. God made it known by sending his angel to his servant John. John gives witness to everything he saw. The things he gives witness to are God's word and what Jesus Christ has said. Blessed is the one who reads the words of this prophecy. Blessed are those who hear it and think everything it says is important. The time when these things will come true is near.

IS EZRA A
MAN OR WOMAN?

What do you think? Most said Ezra's a woman, many said a man, and one even said "an it." The correct answer is . . . he's a man!

God used Ezra in great ways during a very important time in the history of God's people. The books of Ezra and Nehemiah kind of go together. God's people had been captured and sent to live in other countries. The city of Jerusalem had been destroyed. About eighty years after its destruction, some of the people were allowed to go back to Jerusalem to rebuild. When they did, Nehemiah was put in charge of rebuilding the temple. Ezra helped by teaching God's Word to the people there.

Most of you probably haven't read those books, but they really are neat stories. Maybe you could do book reports on them for school or just use them for some extra Bible reading. Here's what the book tells us about Ezra and how God prepared him for his special work. "Ezra had committed himself to study and obey the Law of the Lord. He also wanted to teach the Lord's rules and laws in Israel. Ezra was a priest and teacher. He was an educated man. He knew the Lord's commands and rules for Israel very well" (Ezra 7:10–11).

Ezra was prepared and willing to serve. How is God teaching you to obey, like Ezra? How is God preparing you to serve him? It's such a joy to serve our God! Enjoy!

WHO ARE SOME WOMEN IN THE BIBLE, AND FOR WHAT ARE THEY KNOWN?

What's going on out there? Most couldn't think of any women in the Bible besides Mary, the mother of Jesus, and Mary Magdalene! One place I looked listed more than one hundred. Not all had their names listed, but they were still women noted in the Bible.

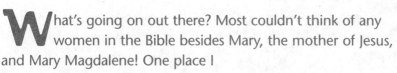

What about Eve (Genesis 2–4)? And there's Sarai/Sarah (Genesis 11–49); Miriam (Exodus 15:10–21); Deborah, the Judge (Judges 5:1–31); Ruth (the book of Ruth); Esther (the book of Esther); widow at Zarephath (1 Kings 17); the prophet Anna (Luke 2:22–40); Lois and Eunice (2 Timothy 1:1–12)—and so many more!

Name three women and girls in your life who are good examples of people who love the Lord. Write their names on the lines below so you can remember to thank them for their faith, and also to pray for them and thank God for them.

_____

_____

_____

WHO ARE SOME "MOMS" IN THE BIBLE?

Since so many kids didn't seem to remember women in the Bible (the last devotion), here's a Dr. Devo quiz about moms in the Bible. The answers are at the bottom of the page.

1. Who was the mother of John the Baptist? (Luke 1:57–60)

    A. Sarah
    B. Elizabeth
    C. Mary Magdalene
    D. Rebecca

2. What mother brought her son a coat every year? (1 Samuel 2:18–21)

    A. Ruth
    B. Hannah
    C. Mary
    D. Sarah

3. Whose mother asked Jesus to grant her sons places at his right and left in heaven? (Matthew 20:20–23)

    A. Peter and Andrew
    B. James and John
    C. Philip and Bartholomew
    D. Nathaniel and Nicodemus

4. Whose mother was paid to be his nurse? (Exodus 2:8–9)

    A. Jesus
    B. Moses
    C. John the Baptist
    D. Samuel

The answer to each one is "B"

BIBLE VERSE
FILL-IN-THE-_____!

"Listen to advice and accept instruction and in the end you will be _____."

And your answer/guess is:

    (A) happy (Kristi)

    (B) smart (Jon)

    (C) in heaven (Eli)

According to Proverbs 19:20, "B" is the closest answer. The word used in the passage is "wise." Is there a difference between smart and wise? What do you think? "Smart" and "wise" are very close to the same thing—usually. But could someone get straight "A's" on his report card every semester and still not be very wise? Wisdom is more than memorizing or knowing answers on a test. It goes deeper. Wisdom will help you make good choices.

So when the writer says to listen to advice and accept instruction so in the end you will be wise, he's reminding you to listen to those who know more than you do. Take the advice of parents and teachers. They probably have more wisdom because they are older and have experienced more. If you accept help, advice, and instruction, you will make good decisions. Following the instruction of God is the very best way to become wise! I guess being called a "wise-guy" isn't a bad thing all the time!

LOL!
(Laughing Out Loud)

Q: What does an envelope say when you lick it?

A: Nothing. It just shuts up.

That's one of Jake's favorite jokes.

In the wise book of Proverbs, the writer uses the word "listen" 17 times. He uses it many times to tell his child to pay attention. He has something important to say. He wants to make sure his son's lips are shut and his ears are open. Proverbs 5:1 is one example, "My son, pay attention to my wisdom, listen well to my words of insight."

It's hard to be quiet sometimes. When is it difficult for you to shut your mouth and just listen? It's important to listen to people God has placed in your life. It's even more important to listen for God's answer to your prayers (even if it's a big ol' no). It's too easy to talk to God but forget to listen for his answers!

For those of you who find it hard not to stop talking . . . Jesus loves to listen to you talk to him. Yes, he wants you to hear what he's saying, but he also has an ear ready to listen to your words. He loves to hear your voice!

BESIDES GOD (JESUS), WHO WAS THE BRAVEST PERSON IN THE BIBLE, AND WHY DO YOU THINK THAT?
(FIRST OF SIX)

These four people were very brave. Pick two or three of them and get someone to guess who they are while you act out something about them. Don't use any words, just actions!

1. Daniel, because of the lions. (Michelle)

2. Mary, because she went through a lot. (Kelsey)

3. Nicodemus. (Carly)

4. Job, because after everything that happened to him, he still praised God. (Kyle)

If you tried doing that acting, you were brave! Some people are scared or shy about acting in front of others.

The Bible contains many examples of bravery. Bravery isn't just about having big muscles. Bravery takes on many different forms. Now pick one or two of the characters above and read their brave stories in the Bible.

Daniel's story is in Daniel 6; part of Mary's brave story is in Luke 1:26–56; the story of Nicodemus is in John 3:1–16; and part of Job's brave story is in Job 1.

BESIDES GOD (JESUS), WHO DO YOU THINK WAS THE BRAVEST PERSON IN THE BIBLE, AND WHY DO YOU THINK THAT? (SECOND OF SIX)

Kirsten gave Peter a standing ovation for his bravery. She told me, "Peter walked on water and even though he didn't have the courage to go all the way to Jesus, he had the courage to try. He was always talking and asking questions which, to me, show bravery. If God came down to earth, I would be all tongue-tied and not know what to say. Peter seemed to always want to know more, therefore he asked Jesus tons of questions."

D.J. and I are giving Kirsten a standing ovation for those awesome words! It takes courage to try difficult things—they may even seem impossible (Matthew 14:22–36). God calls us to be bold and brave when we come to him (Hebrews 4:16). No question is too tough for him to handle. And in John 21:18, Jesus hints that Peter will die by crucifixion. It is believed that Peter was crucified upside down in Rome during the time of Nero. It is said he asked to be upside down because he felt he didn't deserve to die the same way his Savior died for him.

Thanks for sharing, Kirsten. May we be brave in and for Jesus!

294

BESIDES GOD (JESUS), WHO DO YOU THINK WAS THE BRAVEST PERSON IN THE BIBLE, AND WHY DO YOU THINK THAT? (THIRD OF SIX)

Rachel put her vote in for Moses as the bravest because he had to lead a lot of people—about two million! Whoa! That's a lot! Think about all those people waiting for you to make decisions—listening to every word you say. If you said let's go south, they would go south. If you put your right hand on the blue dot, they would—wait, that's another game! Anyway, you get the idea. That would take a lot of bravery. Do you think the leaders in your town, church, school, or country are brave?

Moses, thankfully, knew God was the real leader. Moses could lead all those people as long as he followed God. That's a lesson we need to learn. Do you think other kids see you as a leader? As you grow older, do you think God might want to use you as a leader?

If you are ever called on to lead, remember these things:

1. Rely on God as the real leader—follow his direction; ask for his help, forgiveness, and leadership.

2. Jesus taught that real leadership meant serving—be a servant leader.

Pray this prayer:
"Teach me to do your will, for you are my God; may your good Spirit lead me on level ground" (Psalm 143:10). Amen.

BESIDES GOD (JESUS), WHO DO YOU THINK WAS THE BRAVEST PERSON IN THE BIBLE, AND WHY DO YOU THINK THAT? (FOURTH OF SIX)

Two girls thought the apostle Paul was very brave. Jackie said, "I think Paul was very brave because he kept telling people about Jesus even when they didn't want to hear it and even though he was threatened and put in jail many times." Louisa added to that: "I think that the apostle Paul was the bravest because, after he had been enlightened about how things really were, he went out into the world and spread the Gospel, even among people who might hurt him. He went to prison many times. Still, with God's help, he kept on going."

With that in mind, check out these words written by Paul:

We are pushed hard from all sides. But we are not beaten down. We are bewildered. But that doesn't make us lose hope. Others make us suffer. But God does not desert us. We are knocked down. But we are not knocked out ... We don't give up. Our bodies are becoming weaker and weaker. But our spirits are being renewed day by day. Our troubles are small. They last only for a short time. But they are earning for us a glory that will last forever. It is greater than all our troubles.

2 CORINTHIANS 4:8-9; 16-17 (niRv)

BESIDES GOD (JESUS), WHO DO YOU THINK WAS THE BRAVEST PERSON IN THE BIBLE, AND WHY DO YOU THINK THAT? (FIFTH OF SIX)

Rick voted for Stephen, because he stood up for his faith even to death. Cody said the disciples were brave because they were threatened and still preached the Word of God.

Has anyone ever made fun of you for being a Christian? Maybe. Has anyone hurt you because you stood up for what God said? Possibly. Has anyone tried to kill you because of your faith? Probably not. Stephen, a follower of Jesus, knew what that was like. Stephen was a martyr (pronounced MAR-ter). That is a person who dies for his or her belief. You can read about Stephen in Acts 6:8–8:1.

The religious leaders then made up lies about Stephen and took him to their court. They got so mad at him for telling the truth about Jesus that they dragged him out of the city and threw stones at him until he was dead. While they were throwing the stones, Stephen said, "Lord Jesus, receive my spirit." And just before he died, he said, "Lord, do not hold this sin against them" (Acts 7:59–60). Who else said words like that before his death? (Check out Luke 23:34.)

Be sure to pray for brave followers of Jesus all over the world—those who are being made fun of, hurt, and even killed because of their faith.

I am giving you some special instructions for this devotion. Look down a few lines to see who Abby and Jordan chose as the bravest person from the Bible. Don't say his or her name. Your mission, if you should decide to accept it, is to get others to guess who it is by drawing the story. You have to keep your eyes closed while you're drawing though! Get paper and something to draw with, cover your eyes, and draw away!

Abby and Jordan picked David because he fought a giant and won. He didn't worry that he was too small to make a difference. He used God instead of armor to destroy the giant Goliath.

David faced a giant problem (1 Samuel 17). But he didn't even have to look at Goliath if he didn't want to. God could take care of the problem, using David and his slingshot. Thankfully, David knew how important it was to look to God for help. The king also reminded him of this when he said to David, "Go, and the Lord be with you" (1 Samuel 17:37).

What giant problems are you facing? Be brave by looking to God. Then go, and the Lord be with you!

LOL!
(Laughing Out Loud)

Q: What does Brazil produce more of than any other country?

A: Brazilians.

Get serious now.

Q: What does Christ produce?

A: Christians.

When you look at the word "Christian," do you see the name Christ? Do you think about what that means? Christ produces CHRISTians. Those who follow Christ (and that includes you!) are known as Christians.

Here's the problem: We don't always act or talk or think like Christ, do we? We have been given his name. We have been re-created in him—given a new life. But many times we don't let it show. As you ask Jesus to forgive you for the times you've failed to faithfully wear his name with joy, also ask him to help you so you won't be ashamed to be known by his name—the name that is above all names!

Quick Dr. Devo
Trivia Quiz:

The disciples were first called "Christians" in what town? (The answer is in Acts 11:26)

   (A) Jerusalem

   (B) Ephesus

   (C) Antioch

   (D) New Jersey

If you were asked to cook turkey and stuffing for a Thanksgiving meal for the homeless, how would you cook it?

We were expecting some great recipes but instead, D.J. and I got other interesting answers, like:

- Good. Lovely.

- Mallorie simply said, "I can't cook!"

- Kirsten said, "I'd buy a turkey from the frozen food section, come home and beg my parents to do it for me. When they said no, I would go into the kitchen and stare at it."

- The closest we got to a recipe was from Kayla: "Stuff the turkey with stuffing. Put the turkey in a pan. Put the pan in the oven. Take it out when the popper pops out!"

Even if you can't cook a turkey for a homeless family, you can help in other ways. You may live far away from a city and think no one homeless lives around you.

That may or may not be true. Regardless, someone who is poor or who needs some- thing we take for granted (like food or clothes) surely lives pretty close.

> We know that the earthly tent we live in will be destroyed. But we have a building made by God. It is a house in heaven that lasts forever. Human hands did not build it.
>
> 2 CORINTHIANS 5:1 NIRV

What can you do to help them? You can always pray for them. Lift them up to the one who has a home in heaven for all who place their trust in him—even if they don't have a home on earth . . . yet!

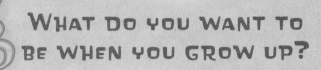

(A) A teacher. I want to teach children what they need to know and why they need to know it. (Sydney)

(B) A doctor, because I can help people. (Shannon)

(C) An insurance man, because my dad is one and it seems fun because he goes on trips and spends a lot of time with me. (Dylan)

(D) A nurse, because you get to take care of babies. (Bethany)

(E) An Air Force pilot to protect people. (Cody)

(F) And a bunch of kids said they want to be veterinarians because they love taking care of animals.

What do all these jobs have in common? If you can't figure that out by just looking at the jobs' names, think about what the reasons have in common?

All these workers care for people or God's creation in some way! It takes a heart like Jesus' heart to care for others. We want to help others because Jesus first helped and loved us. In Psalm 8:4, David asks the Lord, "What is a human being that you think about him? What is a son of man that you take care of him?" (NIRV) But the Lord *does* care about us and calls us to care for other people.

How long do you think it took Mary and Joseph to go from their home in Nazareth to Bethlehem, where Jesus was born?

Kids your age gave me six of these answers. Those weren't quite right, so I added one—the correct answer! Which do you think it is? Here's a hint: Bethlehem is about seventy miles from Nazareth if you travel on a straight road all the way there.

(A) 3 hours

(B) 2 months

(C) 17 days

(D) 87 days

(E) 8 months

(F) about one month

(G) 3 or 4 days, maybe a week

Before I give you the answer, think about this trip. It isn't easy for Mary to walk a long distance because she is very pregnant. Sometimes she can't breathe as easily because the baby is taking so much room inside her body!

Mary and Joseph didn't have planes, trains, or automobiles back then. They either walked or they had a donkey to ride; the Bible doesn't tell us which. So how many of you guessed the longest, "E?" If you did, you were wrong! Ha! Sorry. Just playing with you! The correct answer is "G"—3 to 4 days, maybe a week. It depends on the route, the way Mary handled the trip, and the number of potty breaks they had to take!

It was a rough trip, I'm sure. But Mary and Joseph trusted God. No wonder Mary could sing, "My soul glorifies the Lord and my spirit rejoices in God my Savior (Luke 1:46).

Joy to the World," because it's fun to sing. (Lora)

That *is* a fun song to sing! It's filled with joy! Not only the song is filled with joy . . . the manger is filled with joy, too, and his name is "Jesus!" For hundreds and hundreds of years the world had been waiting for a Savior to be born. And in itty-bitty Bethlehem, in a place where animals are born, we find the world's joy—the promised Messiah. His name is Jesus. What good news of great joy that is for all people (Luke 2:10)!

The song is also a great prayer asking every heart to prepare room for Jesus—the blessed baby, who would be our Savior. None of the innkeepers had a room for him, but you can open your heart and make room for him. Praise the Lord and sing!

Joy to the world, the Lord is come! Let earth receive it's King;
Let ev'ry heart prepare him room. And heav'n and nature sing,
And heav'n and nature sing, And heav'n and heav'n and nature sing!

He rules the world with truth and grace, And makes the nations prove
The glories of his righteousness, And wonders of his love,
And wonders of his love, And wonders, wonders of his love!

WHAT'S YOUR FAVORITE CHRISTMAS SONG?
(SECOND OF THREE)

Go Tell It on the Mountain." (Henry)

This song tells us about the angel's song to the shepherds. It reminds us about what the shepherds did after they saw and worshiped Jesus, the way this passage from the Bible does: "When they had seen him, they spread the word concerning what had been told them about this child, and all who heard it were amazed at what the shepherds said to them" (Luke 2:17–18). The shepherds couldn't keep the good news to themselves! We—you and I—also must tell everyone about Jesus' birth and about what that means for us!

REFRAIN: Go tell it on the mountain,
over the hills and ev'rywhere;
Go tell it on the mountain that Jesus
Christ is born!

While shepherds kept their watching O'er silent flocks by night
Behold, throughout the heavens there shone a holy light.
REFRAIN

The shepherds feared and trembled When lo, above the earth
Rang out the angel chorus That hailed our Savior's birth.
REFRAIN

Down in a lonely manger The humble Christ was born;
And God sent us salvation That blessed Christmas morn.

Away in a Manger"—because it tells of Jesus' birth. (Mandy)

You may want to mark this page so you can use this song as a great prayer at bedtime. The words are very peaceful. Jesus is the Prince of Peace who came to give us peace (Isaiah 9:6). He will stay near us and love us, just as Mary and Joseph stayed close to him and loved him and his heavenly Father watched over him perfectly.

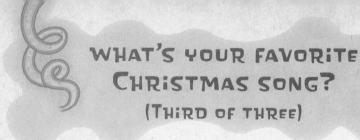

Away in a manger, no crib for a bed,
The little Lord Jesus laid down his sweet head.
The stars in the bright sky looked down where he lay,
The little Lord Jesus asleep on the hay.

The cattle are lowing, the baby awakes,
But little Lord Jesus, no crying he makes.
I love thee, Lord Jesus!
Look down from the sky,
And stay by my cradle until morning is nigh.

Be near me, Lord Jesus; I ask thee to stay
Close by me forever and love me, I pray.
Bless all the dear children in thy tender care,
And take us to heaven to live with thee there.

WHO IS YOUR HERO, AND WHY?
(FIRST OF FOUR)

Let's celebrate these two answers! Both Bethany and Elizabeth said their heroes are their older sisters! That's so awesome! Bethany said she looks up to her sister. (And no, that's not just because her sister is taller!) Elizabeth says her sister is her hero because she's nice to her!

God would love it if brothers and sisters stopped picking on each other in a mean way, bullying each other, making fun of each other, and doing all the other junk brothers and sisters do! God has given us families for love and support. We can learn from family members. If you don't have a brother or sister, remember that the Bible says all followers of Jesus are brothers and sisters in Christ!

Can you think of sisters in the Bible? One was upset at the other one when Jesus visited them. Their story is in Luke 10:38–42. Jesus wanted one to learn from the other. Did you think of Mary and Martha, who were friends of Jesus? Mary sat and learned from Jesus, but Martha cooked and cleaned. Jesus told Martha that Mary had chosen the better thing to do (Luke 10:42).

Maybe you can teach your sister or brother in Christ how important it is to spend time with Jesus every day. Your faith can make a big difference in the lives of your family members. Don't forget, they're watching how you act and what you say! Be a faith hero in your family!

WHO IS YOUR HERO, AND WHY?
(SECOND OF FOUR)

Parents can be awesome heroes for kids. These four kids think so:

1. Kyle says his mom is his hero because she is very nice, and she helps him when he's in trouble.

2. Emiley wrote me saying, "My dad because he is always doing what he believes in and what he thinks is best and LOVES LIFE!"

3. Sam says, "My mom is my hero because she raised my brother and me without help."

4. Christine said her parents are her heroes because they help her through all her troubles.

What a blessing to have Christian parents who love you and the Lord! They take care of you. They make sure you have what you need. They go out of their way for you. They will do anything for you. They hurt when you hurt. They are happy for you when something good happens to you. They want the best for you. What do you love most about *your* parents?

The apostle Paul wrote Timothy, reminding him to be thankful for his faith and the faith of his mother and grandmother. They passed God's Word on to him. Paul wrote, "I have been reminded of your sincere faith, which first lived in your grandmother Lois and in your mother Eunice and, I am persuaded, now lies in you also" (2 Timothy 1:5).

Thank the Lord for faithful hero-parents who love their children and the Lord!

My lab rat, D.J., and I were floored with the insightful answer Louisa, from Moscow, Russia, gave to this question. This 11-year-old wrote, "My hero is the person who is persevering, loves God, will not stop until he has done his best, is positive, can laugh at himself for his mistakes, will always try to help others to be the best they can be, and will stop at nothing to tell the world—or just the people in his neighborhood—about the love of Jesus. Whoever that may be. He is my hero."

Wow! You can say that again, Louisa! I'm so thankful for her awesome faith. I think we *do* need to hear that again!

> I thank God every time I remember you. In all my prayers for all of you, I always pray with joy because of your partnership in the gospel from the first day until now, being confident of this, that he who began a good work in you will carry it on to completion until the day of Christ Jesus.
>
> PHILIPPIANS 1:3–6

"My hero is the person who is persevering, loves God, will not stop until he has done his best, is positive, can laugh at himself for his mistakes, will always try to help others to be the best they can be, and will stop at nothing to tell the world—or just the people in his neighborhood—about the love of Jesus. Whoever that may be. He is my hero."

PSSSssst

309

WHO IS YOUR HERO, AND WHY?
(FOURTH OF FOUR)

Ross and Amanda both mentioned the perfect hero! Ross wrote: "God is my hero because he is always there, he helps me trust in him and most of all he is my Savior." Amanda added that her hero is God because he saved her.

If anyone on earth is your hero, please remember that he or she isn't perfect and could let you down some day. All humans make mistakes. All are sinners, even God's children—though they are forgiven sinners. But God will never let you down. He will never fail you. That's why he is the perfect hero to have.

God, our hero, has an amazing love for us. I love the prayer Paul wrote for the people in the city of Ephesus. It's my prayer for you as you grow in the love of your hero-Savior.

> I pray that he will use his glorious riches to make you strong. May his Holy Spirit give you his power deep down inside you. Then Christ will live in your hearts because you believe in him. And I pray that your love will have deep roots. I pray that it will have a strong foundation. May you have power with all God's people to understand Christ's love. May you know how wide and long and high and deep it is. And may you know his love, even though it can't be known completely. Then you will be filled with everything God has for you.
>
> EPHESIANS 3:16–19 NIrV

WHAT WAS THE HIGH POINT OF YOUR DAY? WHAT WAS THE LOW POINT?

Lord, I call out to you every day.
I lift up my hands to you in prayer.

PSALM 88:9 NIRV

We're going to do something different for this devotion. Let's make this a journal page. You can either write your answers below or talk about them with someone. I'd also encourage you to close with prayer, as the Psalm says. Your two questions are above—about the high and low points of your day.

JOURNAL your thoughts: (Today's date:_____)

_____

_____

_____

_____

_____

_____

_____

_____

_____

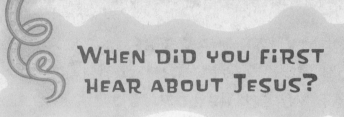

Before we get to Bo's answer I have another question for you! Do you have beautiful feet? Do you know someone who has beautiful feet?

Isaiah 52:7 says, "How beautiful on the mountains are the feet of those who bring good news, who proclaim peace, who bring good tidings, who proclaim salvation, who say to Zion, 'Your God reigns!'" Beautiful feet. Huh?

Here's the scoop: In those days people didn't have cell phones or TV's to get news from the battlefield. Families and town members wanted to know how things were going. So men would run from the battle back home, hopefully bringing good news about a victory. The people watched for a messenger to come over the mountains. It was a beautiful sight to see his feet running toward them with good news. So really anyone who shares good news—especially the good news of Jesus and his love—has beautiful feet.

Let's get back to the question. When did you first hear about Jesus? Bo said that he remembers hearing about him a few years ago from his pastor. Hey Bo, the next time you see your pastor, wouldn't it be fun to tell him he has beautiful feet? I wonder if he will know what you're talking about. If not, be ready to explain!

LOL!
(Laughing Out Loud)

One of Rachel's favorite jokes is:

> Two people were running a race. The one in front turned around and said, "You better catch up or you are going to lose." The other runner said, "I'll ketchup . . . later mustard."

That one runner acted like a real hot dog, eh! Do you like to run? Personally, I'd rather fly around with the help of my trusty jet pack! But whether we like to run or not, the Bible often talks about our Christian lives being a race.

Here's a little Bible Study to help you grow as a runner in the race toward heaven:

1. Read Hebrews 12:1–3. Why do we want to throw off anything that would entangle us, like sin? Where should our eyes be during this faith race? How can we keep from getting tired out?

2. Read Galatians 5:7. What or who has cut in on you during your race to heaven?

3. Read 2 Timothy 4:7–8. What is Paul saying with these words? When Paul wrote these words do you think he was young or old? What does he receive at the end of the race? Is that prize only for him?

See you on the race track, fellow runners! Let's help each other along the way!

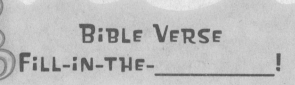

BIBLE VERSE
FILL-IN-THE-_____!

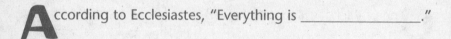

According to Ecclesiastes, "Everything is _____."

The answer I heard most often was, "Everything is possible." Others said:

    (A) "Everything is sinful."

    (B) "Everything is perfect."

    (C) "Everything is God's."

If you look at Ecclesiastes 1:2, you'll find that the answer, according to the one who wrote these words, is really, "Everything is meaningless!" What? That's in the Bible? What does he mean that nothing means anything? Well, the one who wrote this—probably Solomon—spends the entire book, almost twelve chapters, telling us that life is meaningless. He says we do this and that, but what's the purpose. In the end we die. He complains. He whines. He throws his arms up in the air! But then he ends the book—the last two verses of the last chapter—by telling us his point. After all that, he tells us that nothing has meaning . . . without God.

He writes, "And here's the final thing I want to say. Have respect for God and obey his commandments. That's what everyone should do" (Ecclesiastes 12:13 NIrV). Do you want your life to have meaning? Make sure your Savior is right smack dab in the middle of everything you do!

ABOUT HOW MANY PEOPLE WERE BAPTIZED ON THE DAY OF PENTECOST IN ACTS 2?

If you've seen a number of people baptized at your church, what's the most you've seen at one time? After Jesus ascended into heaven, Jewish families from all over the world traveled to Jerusalem to celebrate an Old Testament festival called Pentecost.

While all these people were in Jerusalem, the disciples received the gift of the Holy Spirit. They were able to speak in the languages of those who had come from all over the world. So what do you think they said? Yep! The disciples told them about Jesus and how he came to save the world. Many people believed in Jesus as their Savior then, and many were baptized that day. So how many were baptized? One of these answers that kids gave me is correct—which one do you think it is?

(A) 67

(B) 2235

(C) 100

(D) 3000

(E) 172

(F) 5 billion

Here's the answer from Acts 2:41. After the disciple Peter finished preaching, it says that "Those who accepted his message were baptized, and about three thousand were added to their number that day."

That's a growing church! Pray that more people throughout the world come to know him every day!

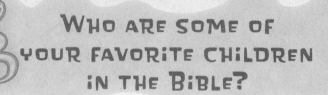

WHO ARE SOME OF YOUR FAVORITE CHILDREN IN THE BIBLE?

While many kids said David was a favorite, Brandon was the only one to mention Samuel. Sammy boy has a good story to tell, and God has a great story to tell through Samuel's life. It all started when Sam was a child. (Isn't that where it usually starts?)

You see, Sam's mom, Hannah, really wanted children, but she wasn't able to have any. So she prayed and prayed and prayed. She told God that if she could have a child, she would give him back to the Lord for his service. God allowed her to become pregnant, and Hannah gave birth to a son. (That's where Samuel comes in.)

After a few years of raising Samuel, Hannah took Samuel to the house of the Lord and presented him to the priest, Eli. Hannah said to Eli, "I prayed for this child, and the Lord has granted me what I asked of him. So now I give him to the Lord. For his whole life he will be given over to the Lord" (1 Samuel 1:27–28). Those words are followed by a beautiful prayer Hannah offered to God in 1 Samuel 2:1–11.

That's quite a way for the life of a little boy to start! But wait! There's more! I'm going to have you dig around 1 Samuel 3:1–19 to discover the wonderful story about the Lord calling Sammy-boy! Have fun digging and learning!

IF YOU COULD ASK JUDAS ANYTHING, WHAT WOULD YOU ASK?

The disciple Judas betrayed Jesus and handed him over to be crucified. He did it for thirty silver coins (Matthew 26:14–16), (about four months' pay for most workers.) Afterward, he felt bad about what he had done, but he didn't repent. He killed himself instead. So many questions could be asked. Here are some from kids:

- Abby would ask, "Was the money worth it?" People ask that question all the time after they get greedy.

- Ben said he'd ask, "How did it feel to sell someone?" That's really what Judas did. He sold his Savior.

- Jackie has a one word question that asks so much, "Why?"

- Christine has a tough one: "Why did you hang yourself rather than ask for forgiveness?" Sometimes people think there is no hope—they can't go on. They forget to trust in the help and forgiveness of Jesus. But we already knew one of Jesus' followers wouldn't make it to heaven because he didn't turn to Jesus (Psalm 41:9 and John 17:12).

- And even though this is a serious subject, Rick's answer made me smile. Rick would ask, "What were you *thinking*?"

God used this and the death of Jesus for our good—to save the world. He's so awesome!

WHAT'S YOUR FAVORITE THING TO DO WITH YOUR FRIENDS?

- Shop! (Ally)

- Talk! (Jackie)

- I like to talk about our favorite books and play with animals, like my friend's dog, Mackey. (Rachel)

- Go fishing, play soccer, and talk online. (James)

- Play basketball. (Kirsten)

- Swim. (Michelle)

- Play tag! (Corey)

Friends are wonderful gifts from God. I'm glad God has given you as a friend to me! Even if we haven't met, I feel like we're friends! And one day we'll meet in heaven! Until that time, we can enjoy doing things with our friends—things outside, things inside; having fun at school or in the neighborhood; praying together and playing together; laughing and maybe even crying together; and worshiping God in church and at recess! Friends are gifts from heaven!

I hope you can live the words of Proverbs 17:17: "A friend loves at all times." Thank the Lord for faithful friends and friends that have placed their faith in him! Have fun together!

WHAT'S THE LAST WORD IN THE BIBLE?

Most kids got the answer to this question correct. The last word in the Bible is "Amen." The last verse reads, "The grace of the Lord Jesus be with God's people. Amen" (Revelation 22:21).

Do you know what the word "Amen" means? We use it at the end of prayers, but it doesn't mean, "The End!" And no, it doesn't mean, "Over and out, God." It means, "So be it." or "So shall it be." If you knew that already, do you think about that when you say "amen" at the end of your prayers? If you didn't know that before I hope you'll think about its meaning now.

We pray and then say, "So be it, God! I'm leaving it in your hands. I praised your name. I gave you my requests. I asked for forgiveness. Now I give it all to you. So be it. Your will be done!"

It's cool to think in that way when we end a prayer. But now think about it as the ending to the whole Bible! Everything from "In the beginning God . . ." through Eden to sin; from judges and kings; through wars and rumors of wars; from the birth of Jesus to his death to his resurrection to his ascension into heaven; from the Great Commission to Pentecost; from the acts of the apostles to the epistles to the revelation about heaven!" Amen! So be it! Let this all be to your glory, God. And the grace of the Lord Jesus be with God's people! (That's you and me!) Amen! Amen! Amen!

One Final Question!

OH NO! We're at the end of another Dr. Devo devotion book! Hand me a tissue! The tears are flowing! This has been great fun! I hope you've learned things and grown in your faith. I have!

I loved interviewing kids, asking them questions about this and that. You've seen the questions and their answers on every page of this book. But there's one more question, and it comes from Jesus. It's the same question Jesus once asked his disciple, Simon Peter. Are you ready? You need to answer. In fact, it's a matter of life or death! Yes, it's that big a deal! Here we go!

The question Jesus has for you is this: "Who do you say I am?" Peter answered it this way, "You are the Christ, the Son of the living God." Is that your answer, too? Can you say that out loud right now, believing it in your heart? I pray you will. Go ahead . . . I can wait the rest of your lifetime to hear the answer, but I hope you say it believing now. Who do you say Jesus is?

It's such an important question. How you answer it tells about your relationship with Jesus, your Savior. Do you believe in Jesus as your personal, life-giving Savior? Do you believe he's the only way to heaven? If so, I say "AMEN!" I can't wait to see you in heaven! Thanks, my friends, for sharing this time with me, with D.J., and most importantly, with Jesus!